The Professional Potter

The Professional Potter

BY THOMAS SHAFER

WATSON-GUPTILL PUBLICATIONS, NEW YORK
PITMAN PUBLISHING, LONDON

Opposite page: Willy and Elly Kuch. Plate
with wax-resist decoration (see page 125).

Copyright© 1978 by Watson-Guptill Publications

First published 1978 in the United States and Canada by Watson-Guptill Publications,
a division of Billboard Publications, Inc.,
1515 Broadway, New York, N.Y. 10036

Published in Great Britain by Pitman Publishing Ltd.,
39 Parker Street, London WC2B 5PB
ISBN 273-01279-7

Library of Congress Cataloging in Publication Data
Shafer, Thomas, 1937–
   The professional potter.
   Bibliography: p.
   Includes index.
   1. Pottery. 2. Potters—Interviews. I. Title.
HD9610.5.S47 1978   338.7'61'73830922   78-16547
ISBN 0-8230-4417-3

Manufactured in U.S.A.

First Printing, 1978

To Yvonne

PREFACE

Stephen Jepson. Plates decorated with wax-resist brushwork designs in red, blue, and orange over a white glaze.

In the current economic environment of the United States, England, and West Germany it is quite possible to make a comfortable living as an independent studio potter. Over the last twenty years, increasing middle-class affluence coupled with a growing interest in the arts, especially in the United States, has made it possible for a growing number of potters to support themselves and their families through selling their work. The life of an independent craftsman has an undeniable romantic appeal and can be very rewarding, but requires self-discipline, dedication, and long hours of hard work.

The British, American, and German potteries in this book have been selected for the quality and variety of their work and for the range of different approaches in terms of attitudes and goals, studio organization, work cycles, assistants, sales, and the types of work produced. All of these potters make a living by producing mostly functional ware, and share a deep commitment to making technically sound, carefully crafted pots as well as to developing their own artistic potential. Although there is a wide range in age, all are well established and highly successful in terms of their own concepts of success, and in relation to the goals they have set for themselves. All live comfortably in pleasant surroundings, but there is a wide range of income, reflecting individual temperament and preference in manner of working, scale of production, number of assistants, and way of living. These six potteries cannot be considered typical since each has evolved from a unique combination of background, financial circumstances, personalities, goals, and chance. However, they do illustrate certain attitudes, approaches, and ways of working that appear in different combinations and proportions in many other potteries.

The method of selling is an important influence on the operation of a pottery and on the pots themselves (and vice versa), and each of these potters has very definite ideas on sales methods. A crucial decision is whether to sell directly to retail customers or through shops and galleries. Wholesaling means a smaller profit on each piece, while direct retail sales mean a larger investment of time. Most potters elect to do both in varying proportions. An important direct sales outlet for many American potters has been the art fair, a phenomenon dating back to about 1950, but which has burgeoned only in the last 15 years. Art fairs or craft fairs are usually organized to benefit a school, museum, or charitable cause, while some are private profit-making enterprises, and others are run as a service to artists and as public relations events. There is an entry fee for exhibitors, and sometimes the public is charged an admission fee, and a few fairs also take a percentage of sales. Artists set up their own displays and handle their own sales. Most fairs last from one to three days. The best fairs attract thousands of interested buyers, and are juried to maintain standards and a manageable size. There are so many fairs that a potter could (and many do) sell most of his production in this way.

In preparing this book I visited each of the six studios and photographed the potters at work as well as individual examples of their pottery. The information is based on taped interviews, informal conversations and observation of the studios in operation, as well as an acquaintance with the work of these potters for several years.

I would like to express my gratitude to the potters who worked with me on this project for their cooperation and hospitality during the interviews and photographing, and for providing additional photographs, answering numerous questions that came up during the writing, and reading the manuscript and suggesting alterations. I would like to thank my editors, Sarah Bodine, with whom the idea was conceived, and Jennifer Place and Donna Wilkinson, with whom the work was completed, and the designer, Bob Fillie. Finally, special thanks to my wife Yvonne for her encouragement and advice, and for typing the manuscript.

Michael and Sheila Casson photographs on pages 32, 36, and 38 by Marc Nisbet; Karl Christiansen photographs on pages 54 (bottom), and 67 by Greg Gradient and page 60 (top) by Russ Munn; John Glick photographs on frontis, back cover, pages 69, 70, 73, 74, 76, 77 (top), 78, 81 (bottom), 82 (top), 83, 84, 86, 88, and 90 (bottom) by Bob Vigiletti; Stephen Jepson photographs on opposite page by Raymond Gendreau. Most other photographs are by the author.

John Glick. Teapot with slab body formed in press mold, thrown rim and lid, press-molded spout, and wire-cut handle with modeled details.

CONTENTS

A group of planters and small sculptures enlivens a corner of the garden next to the Kuchs studio.

ALAN CAIGER-SMITH

Aldermaston Pottery

ALDERMASTON, BERKSHIRE, ENGLAND

Left
Alan usually paints spontaneously without guidelines. Here, he paints a precise design in a commemorative bowl.

Right
Pedestaled, covered jar with gold lustre decoration.

Since 1955 Alan Caiger-Smith has operated the Aldermaston Pottery, where he makes tin-glazed earthenware (majolica)—a medium that few contemporary artist-potters use. He currently employs six other potters, who work with him and produce a wide range of brush-decorated domestic ware (both repeat and individual work) as well as special commissions.

The pottery is located in the center of Aldermaston, a tiny village of old red brick tile-roofed houses nestled in the lush green valley of the Kennet River about 50 miles west of London. Alan lives with his wife and four teenage sons in an 18th-century farmhouse about two miles from the pottery. Rustic yet elegant, the house stands magnificently alone at the end of a narrow lane, surrounded by fields and woods. Both the house and studio seem idyllic, almost removed from the 20th century, which intrudes only in the form of occasional trucks, roaring through the village past the studio.

Because he is deeply interested in the history of tin-glaze pottery, Alan has visited surviving traditional production centers in England, Holland, Spain, Italy, and Egypt as well as museums all over Europe. He also has written a carefully researched and eloquent book on tin-glaze pottery in Europe and the Islamic world. Enriched by his experience and insight as a potter, the book traces the development of the tin-glaze tradition from its origins in the Middle East, through its evolution in Spain, Italy, and Northern Europe, up to the present time.

He has given lecture-demonstrations, but Alan has never done

regular teaching since he feels it would take too much time away from the pottery.

BACKGROUND

Although interested in painting, Alan Caiger-Smith studied history and English literature at King's College, Cambridge. He had, however, previously studied painting for a year at Camberwell School of Art in London and developed an amateur interest in pottery during his years at Cambridge. At the age of 22, on a trip to Spain when he saw potters making traditional majolica ware at Triana, he began to think of combining his interests in painting and pottery.

For the next two years Alan lived in London, and with the goal of learning to make tin-glazed earthenware he took evening pottery classes at the Central School in 1954. However, English potters at that time were almost totally committed to the Oriental stoneware tradition, and most of Alan's practical and technical expertise in majolica had to be developed through experience.

Though he now looks back on his work of that time as far from competent, by 1955 he had determined to set up his own studio. After searching for a suitable location in or near London, he finally chose a former blacksmith shop in the village of Aldermaston, Berkshire, where he had been brought up. The 18th-century brick building had been unoccupied for more than three years, had no electricity, limited plumbing, and required extensive repairs, but was rehabilitated while retaining the rustic beauty of the original structure.

For the first year Alan worked alone, gradually developing his skill and increasing sales. He was then joined by another potter, who worked with him until 1960, when he left to start his own studio. By this time Alan felt established and confident enough to hire three new people and began to develop the kind of group organization he had envisioned from the beginning.

Alan:
When I began it was very tempting financially to take on some teaching, but it seemed to me a temptation to be resisted, because the pottery always needs as much time, energy, and imagination as I can give it. I think in the long run it was the right decision to concentrate on the pottery rather than divide my time and energy.

The back of the studio overlooks a garden and orchard. The old studio is in the center, at left the adjoining cottage, and at right a corner of the new studio.

STUDIO AND EQUIPMENT

The studio space has more than doubled since 1955, but the former blacksmith shop remains the center of activity. From the front the studio appears to be one of the red brick, tile-roofed cottages closely lining the road through the village of Aldermaston, and is identified only by an inconspicuous sign "The Pottery" and a few pots displayed in a small window.

The working area is oriented toward the back where large windows open onto a tiny patio that separates the old studio from a new one built in 1974. The first floor of the old studio is divided into two areas, one for throwing, trimming, and assembling pots, the other for decorating, storage, and packing. The walls are lined with shelves that hold hundreds of green and bisque pots, and banks of shelves surround a small electric kiln. Three Leach-type treadle wheels are lined up under a large window, and the old brick forge, covered over, forms a massive work table.

A steep narrow stair leads to the bright, spacious second floor, which is the display and sales area. Shelves and tables are laden with pots; mugs and pitchers hang from walls and beams; and an overflow of bowls is spread on the floor under tables. The profusion of so many brightly decorated pots is almost overwhelming, but everything is neatly and logically arranged. Curtained storage shelves and a loft are filled with hundreds of pieces, representing

Above
Part of the original studio.

Jacki Rothery, an assistant, attaches handles to casseroles.

13

A small part of the extensive wood store with the kiln in the background.

Ready to be bricked up, the kiln is packed with glazed ware. Only a small portion of the load can be seen through the narrow door.

various forms, decorations, or colors. These are not for sale, but are used as samples to show customers or as references for the potters themselves.

The new studio, a simple one-story brick structure that was largely built by Alan and the other potters with the help of a local builder, was completed in 1974. In addition to a spacious work area with large windows overlooking a garden, orchard, and the countryside beyond, there are clay preparation and storage areas, a glaze area, extensive shelving for pots awaiting decorating or firing, and a small room for tools and parts needed for maintenance and repairs. Equipment includes two wheels and a pug mill. Although the red clay is bought in the ready-to-use plastic state, the pug mill is used for reprocessing scrap and for blending in sand to make an ovenware body. Adjoining the new studio at the back is the kiln shed, open on two sides, which houses the wood kiln. Behind this is a long storage shed where wood for the kiln is neatly stacked.

The cottage adjoining the pottery on one side is owned by Alan, and two of his employees live there. An upstairs room of this cottage, entered through the showroom, serves as Alan's office.

Across the road, Alan also owns another cottage where one of his assistants, Edgar Campden, and his family live. Behind this cottage a barn houses a small studio used by Edgar and a separate room containing a wheel and jiggering and jolleying equipment for making some tableware (plates and small mugs). Jiggering and jolleying are mechanical methods for forming simple shapes from soft clay by means of a spinning plaster mold and a pivoted lever fitted with a metal template. This system allows a relatively unskilled worker to reproduce given forms accurately and rapidly.

The second floor of the barn serves as a storage area and informal gallery where pots are kept for exhibitions. From each firing some outstanding pieces are selected for this collection, in order to always have the best work on hand to form the nucleus of an exhibition. About 90 percent of these pots are individual work, although particularly successful standard repeat pieces are occasionally included.

Kilns. At first Alan did all his firing in a small electric kiln, but by 1960, with the production of four potters to fire, it became obvious that a much larger kiln was needed. Since there was insufficient current in the village to operate a larger electric kiln, it was clear that an alternate fuel would have to be used. Alan considered oil, gas, even coal. A cheap, convenient fuel supply was available in the form of reject willow wood from local cricket bat plantations, and this was a deciding factor in choosing to build a wood-fired kiln.

Alan had always believed that the traditional way of firing tin glaze in an oxidizing atmosphere was best. However, he discovered that a light intermittent reduction, unavoidable in his first wood kiln, produced delightful effects that actually favored the development of some colors, produced variations unobtainable by oxidation, and gave added depth and richness to the glaze. The present wood kiln, designed by Alan and built in 1964, has 170 cubic feet of stacking space. It is used for about twelve glaze firings and four lustre firings per year, as well as about half of the bisque firings. The electric kilns are used for bisque, for glaze firings since certain colors develop best by oxidation, and for high-temperature firing of the small amount of porcelain produced.

Large bowl with decoration in red-gold lustre, 16'' (41 cm) in diameter.

Small bowl painted in gold-and-red lustres.

The glaze firing cycle in the wood kiln is about 14 hours at 1050°C to 1060°C, after an overnight pre-heating with gas to drive out moisture. An oxidizing atmosphere is carefully maintained until the later stages of the firing, when intermittent reduction is begun. With the dampers properly adjusted, a brief period of light reduction naturally occurs as each new charge of fuel is added, but clears up within 15 to 25 seconds. The reduction is carefully controlled to avoid blistering of the lead glazes, which can easily result from reducing too heavily or for too long.

A lustre firing must be planned to follow immediately after unloading a bisque or glaze firing so the kiln is completely dry, since any moisture in the kiln vaporized during the firing could dissolve some of the lustre pigment. The lustres are applied in the form of metallic salts (mixed with ochre in an oily medium) over already-fired glazed ware. In a third firing to low red heat in a smoky reduction atmosphere, a thin film of irridescent metal is fused onto the glaze surface. The lustres are fired in a clean oxidizing atmosphere up to the maximum temperature of 670°C (about 6½ hours), followed by a 20-minute soaking period and finally about 50 minutes of smoky reduction with the temperature remaining constant. The development of the lustres is checked by using small clay test rings that bear the same glaze and lustres as the pots. The rings are lined up behind a spyhole and drawn out one by one with a metal rod at several stages during the reduction period to determine when the lustres have properly developed. When removed from the kiln after cooling, the pots are covered with soot and powdery ochre that is rubbed away to reveal the metal.

Because of the limited information available when Alan began working with reduced lustres in 1962, a great deal of experimentation and failure preceded his first successes. He fired a small test kiln 26 times before beginning to obtain any good results. Now, despite his considerable experience with lustre firing, Alan still finds it unpredictable, and even in a good firing only about 80 percent of the pots are likely to be successful, while in a bad firing 60 percent might be seconds or wasters. Such a high rate of loss is redeemed financially by higher prices for the lustre-ware and spiritually by the unique beauty of the best pieces.

Jason Shackleton, an assistant, assembles a group of teapots.

ASSISTANTS

From the beginning Alan Caiger-Smith's goal was to establish a studio where he would employ several potters to work together on all phases of production: making standard ware and individual pieces, and sharing the other jobs such as mixing clay and glazes, loading and firing kilns, and handling sales. The number of assistants has varied from three in 1960 to as many as ten, but Alan has concluded that seven can most comfortably and efficiently utilize his facilities and work most cohesively as a team. At present there are six potters working with Alan. One assistant, Edgar Campden, has been with him for 16 years, while the others have all joined the pottery during the last four years. Most have come with some previous experience in throwing, and some were already proficient, but few have had experience in painted decoration.

The assistants come from all over England, and there have been at various times two Australians, a Czech, and an American working in the studio as well. All the potters find places to live near the pottery; four of them live in cottages owned or rented by Alan.

Because most assistants stay for several years, openings occur infrequently, and there are always many applicants. Alan chooses new trainees on the basis of enthusiasm, attitude, potential, and compatibility with the group as much as for their demonstrable skill, and indeed some have had almost no experience with clay.

Trainees are paid from the beginning, even though at first they may not contribute directly to production. They can do many other jobs in the studio as they are learning. Alan calculates that during the first year a new trainee will probably be paid more than he brings in, but as his skill develops this will be compensated for during the second year, even though his pay will also have increased.

There are no written contracts. A new assistant is taken on for a one-month trial period, after which a verbal agreement is made. Alan feels very strongly that to keep someone who no longer wanted to stay would be destructive to the group feeling he has worked to achieve; likewise, to keep someone who he felt was not doing good work or was disrupting the group effort would be unacceptable.

Alan is very much involved in the training of each new potter, especially in brushwork, but the trainee also learns from the most experienced employees. Presently there is only one first-year potter, while two others are in their second year. Alan plans and assigns work to each potter, and each person is involved in all phases of production. Alan always knows who is doing what, and whether the job is one he is familiar with or one in which he may need help or supervision. From the beginning, everyone does both throwing and decorating.

Trainees invariably produce a high percentage of seconds at first, often spoiling a well-made pot with badly done decoration. Learning through experience and mistakes, however, they are soon able to consistently produce the simplest of the repeat forms and brushwork designs, and gradually master the complex ones.

For the first year or so people are not familiar enough with the techniques and firing effects to produce acceptable individual work. When they have mastered the standard forms and decoration, they begin to do some free work, which usually begins as variations of the repeat ware. Occasionally these variations may themselves be developed as prototypes for new repeat ware.

Most of the potters have ideas of their own, and these may be followed up on their own time, provided they can be realized with the existing studio materials and equipment. Such pieces may be fired, with the potter paying the cost of materials and firing. These pots become the potter's property and are not sold through the studio.

Most of the special commission work is executed by Alan or Edgar, but some orders may be assigned to the other experienced people.

WORK CYCLES

There are essentially no work cycles, since all phases of production are carried on simultaneously and shelves are normally filled with large numbers of pots in various stages of completion. A kind of cyclic feeling is generated, however, by the wood kiln firings, which represent a periodic culmination of effort. A monthly glaze firing and four lustre firings per year are infrequent enough to make each one an event, and large enough (perhaps 500 pots)

Edgar Campden decorates a small hanging pot using one of the standard motifs.

A corner of the second-floor showroom.

so a successful outcome is of great importance. The process of loading takes two days, and a 14-hour glaze firing requires the energy and continual attention of several people working in three-hour shifts at stoking. Either Alan or Edgar is always involved in the important final hours of a firing to make critical decisions and cope with any problems that may arise.

A normal workday is from eight to five with a lunch break and morning and afternoon tea breaks. The atmosphere is relaxed and the pace unhurried but steady. All the potters work a 40-hour week, but there is usually some activity evenings and weekends as well, when they work on their own ideas or do piecework for extra pay.

Alan establishes the production goals and assigns work to each potter based on his individual skills and capabilities. Edgar helps with supervision of day-to-day details and demonstrations for the trainees. The potters are trained in both throwing and painting, eventually becoming proficient in all of the repeat forms and decorative patterns. Each potter usually alternates between two or three weeks at the wheel and a similar period with the brush, almost always decorating those pieces he made himself.

To keep the pottery running smoothly and to enable everyone to participate fully in the making of pots, each assistant is assigned specific jobs such as clay and glaze preparation, handling sales, keeping the showroom in order, putting together shop orders, packing for shipment, maintenance of equipment, taking care of the wood supply, etc. Just as Alan has found that seven potters is an optimum number for his facilities and the kind of interaction he wants, he feels that he has achieved a comfortable

Alan:
A working routine or pattern gives you continuity, and continuity is strength and very often enjoyment. But it is important occasionally to break the routine because there is a subtle difference between a continuity that becomes binding and a continuity that makes for a good flow. An interruption now and again puts you on your mettle, wakes you up, draws out of you something that doesn't come quite so easily, and you break new ground.

19

Two jars inspired by Spanish and Italian drug jars (albarello) of the 14th and 15th centuries. This one (left) by Edgar Campden, is 11″ (28 cm) high. Jar (right) by Alan Caiger-Smith, 11″ (28 cm) high.

degree of organization that permits smooth and efficient functioning without becoming stifling or inflexible.

In making repeat ware, a working rhythm or pattern is important, not only for efficiency of production, but for the enjoyment of his work, and ultimately for the quality of the pots. But Alan welcomes the break from routine provided by special commissions, which have often forced him to think and grow in new directions.

SALES

Direct retail sales from the studio showroom make up a substantial portion of the total, but several galleries and shops in England as well as in Australia and New Zealand are also regularly supplied. At one time Alan sent pottery to some shops on a sale-or-return (consignment) basis, receiving payment for the pots only after the shop had sold them. Because of the additional book-keeping and possible confusion, Alan prefers not to sell in this

way and no longer finds it necessary. Currently he gives shops
only a 10 percent discount below his normal retail prices, and the
shop markup results in somewhat higher retail prices than those
charged at the pottery. Still, there are enough buyers on those
terms to take as much work as can be spared while maintaining a
reasonable inventory for sale at the studio.

During the first few years, before Alan had established a repu-
tation, few customers came to the studio, and they were mostly
acquaintances or people who had seen the shop by chance. Con-
sequently, very little was sold at the pottery except for seconds or
small things such as mugs. Most of the work was sold to shops
(one in London and one in Colorado were the most regular outlets) and through exhibitions. Gradually, as Alan's work became
known, more customers found their way to Aldermaston, and orders from shops greatly increased as well. In fact, demand for
some types of pots, especially ovenware, is now sometimes too
great, and Alan has found himself forced to refuse orders for

Left
Commissioned goblets incorporating lettering in the decoration, painted in blue-green, orange, green, purple, and brown, 6″ (15.2 cm) high.

Below left
Standard ware pitcher.

Below
Standard ware teapot.

some of the best-selling items in order to maintain a variety and balance in production.

The showroom at the pottery is kept well stocked with a full range of repeat and individual work that is continually changing, which encourages customers to return often. Alan estimates that 75 percent of the studio customers return several times a year, and this includes many who come considerable distances.

Alan concedes he is influenced in some details of his work by what sells best, but essentially follows his own direction.

One of the latter was the reduced lustres, which required a great deal of experimentation, resulted in a high percentage of loss in firing, and were initially difficult to sell. Now Alan's lustreware is regarded by many as his most spectacularly beautiful work, and lustre pieces are easily sold for twice the price of comparable non-lustre pieces.

Pricing. Pricing is generally based on four factors: size, firing risks, time required for making, and time required for painting. This may be modified by judgments of relative quality in pieces that are significantly above or below the norm.

More or less standard prices have been established for the 120 different shapes of repeat ware, but pieces that are flawed or not up to standard are priced down and sold as seconds or learners' pieces, while successful pots are marked with a star and priced up. A few years ago Alan made a systematic analysis of the time required for making and painting the repeat items and kept a record of the number of each sold during a year. On the basis of this study he determined that some things had been underpriced in relation to others, with respect to the time and work involved, and prices were adjusted accordingly.

In pricing free individual work, which is so much more varied, prices are more approximate, and quality judgments are a more significant factor. The best pieces may be three to four times the price of average pots of similar size, type, and decoration. Lustreware, because of the additional firing and the higher rate of loss due to the unpredictability of the lustre firing, is normally priced about twice as high as comparable non-lustre pieces.

Most difficult to price are the pieces sent to exhibitions. Because these are selected from pots set aside as superior, their prices are determined somewhat subjectively, based on relative merit.

ANALYSIS OF WORK

The production of the Aldermaston pottery consists mainly of functional domestic ware: mugs, jars, pitchers, vases, goblets, plates, bowls, tureens, and ovenware. About 75 percent of the production is standard repeat ware, most of it designed by Alan. Of the remaining 25 percent, about half is free, individual work in the studio style, while the other half is commission work, including sets of dinnerware, commemorative plates, tiles, lamps, murals, liturgical pieces such as altar crosses, candelabra, and even baptismal fonts.

Most of the approximately 120 standard repeat shapes are wheel thrown, but a few forms are slab-built or combinations of slab and thrown elements; while others, such as the square dishes and rectangular platters, are formed with plaster press molds. Jiggering and jolleying equipment is used to make small mugs and three sizes of plates, since this method greatly increases the out-

Alan:
I am a bit influenced by what sells, but not very much. I have always felt that if you do what pleases you, and do it as well as you can, other people who share the same outlook will come and find it. I think the life history of this pottery has proved that point. Over the 21 years I've been going, I have turned down quite a lot of things that could have been sold very easily, and have embarked on quite a lot of things that certainly did not sell easily.

put of these pieces for which uniformity and speed of production are important, while enabling Alan to retain precise control of the design and quality.

There is no catalog, but many of the repeat designs have names or numbers and can be ordered, and photographs or actual examples of these are kept for reference. Even the repeat ware evolves and changes over the years, however, and Alan feels that it is important for the workshop to retain the freedom to make such changes.

Standard wheel-thrown forms of average size are usually made in groups or series of one to four dozen. Alan believes strongly in the value of repetition throwing, which when done attentively leads to a gradual evolution and perfection of form, through subtle almost imperceptible changes. Individual free work that usually evolves from variations on standard ware is also important to the healthy functioning of the pottery and to the development of the individual potters. Repeat designs establish a common vocabulary and style, which is followed with numerous variations in the individual work, from which, in turn, new ideas for repeat work often come. The repeat work sets a standard and gives the group continuity, stability, and unity of purpose, while the free work develops originality and individuality within the studio style.

Alan:
Our idea is that repeat work and free work should help each other. This entails keeping a balance between them, and trying to insure that the regular commitments of the workshop do not squeeze out the time needed for new work, or vice versa.

Glazes and Decoration. Except for a small amount of porcelain, all of the Aldermaston pottery is made from a smooth red earthenware clay from Devon. Various clear and colored glazes are occasionally used, but almost all the work is glazed opaque white as a background for the brush decoration. Lead is used as a flux in the glazes, but the pots are absolutely safe to use since the glazes have been properly compounded and fired to minimize lead release. All have been tested and are well within government safety standards. Six different white glazes are used, all opacified with tin oxide, but varying in texture and in the way they react with the coloring oxides of the painted decoration. Because of the low-temperature firing a wonderful range of bright clear colors is possible. Mixtures of cobalt, iron, manganese, chrome, copper, nickel, tin, antimony, and vanadium are used to produced blue, blue-green, magenta, mauve, orange, yellow, green, and brown. Many of the simpler pieces are decorated in only one or two colors, while others employ three or more. The reduction-fired lustres provide a whole other range of colors and textures with elusive metallic reflections of gold, yellow, orange, and red. Flashing, a local reduction of the glaze, sometimes produces a soft, darkened halo around the brushwork of the lustre decoration, which seems to intensify its brilliance.

Aside from the texture and color of majolica, which is in itself unusual to the stoneware-accustomed eye, the distinguishing feature of Aldermaston pottery is the brush decoration. The crisp, clear style of painting developed by Alan is based on a quick, precise, yet flowing brushwork, employing various types of brushes for particular strokes that are natural to them. About a dozen types and sizes are used, including broad square-ended sign painters' brushes, fine pointed brushes, and bamboo-handled Japanese brushes, and as many as six different brushes might be used in executing a single complex design. To prepare the dry pigments for painting, they are ground on a tile with a palette knife, working in small amounts of water and gum arabic to ob-

The decoration on each of these three bowls is based on a tripartite division of space, but the lively spontaneous brush-work is completely different in each one.

Bowl painted in browns and black with sgraffito details, 13″ (33 cm) in diameter.

Bowl with brush decoration in red lustre.

Bowl with direct brushwork and wax-resist, 13″ (33 cm) diameter.

Bird made from a basic thrown form, altered and with additions, painted in red lustre.

Large covered jar painted in silvery-yellow lustre with sgrafitto details, 14″ (36 cm) high.

tain the proper brushing consistency. Because of the powdery, absorbent surface of the unfired glaze on which the painting is done, individual brushstrokes are fairly short, to avoid running out of color in mid stroke. There is a beautiful natural rhythm in the style that retains freshness and vitality along with its crisp precision.

Brush decoration is sometimes enriched with sgraffito details in the form of fine lines scratched through the colorant to expose the glaze. Though most decoration is direct brushwork, wax resist is also used. The pattern is painted in wax emulsion on the raw glaze, and the colorant, which is applied over the wax with a broad brush, adheres only to the unwaxed areas, reserving the design in white.

The style of painting followed by the other potters, as well as the specific patterns on repeat ware, have been clearly established by Alan. There is a high level of consistency and quality in the painting of repeat ware, although variations in the fluency of brushwork can be seen. In the freer, individual work, the difference seems greater; the other potters rarely approach the vitality, mastery, and inventiveness of Alan's work, which ranges from spare compositions of a few sinuous lines to lush complex ones, contrasting broad, bold strokes with delicate details and staccato accents.

Alan's spirited and lyrical style is free and lively, yet disciplined and controlled, obviously influenced by historical precedents (notably Middle Eastern and Hispano-Moresque tin-glaze ware) yet uniquely his own. The rich and varied repertoire of brushstrokes, evolved from an intimate understanding of the characteristics and potential of his brushes, is not merely facile, but is combined with a sophisticated and inventive sense of form and pattern and an expressive sincerity. Alan usually paints without sketches or guidelines, preferring the more spontaneous quality of a design developed with the brush directly from an idea existing only in his mind.

His technique is admirably suited to his materials and firing. A stoneware reduction fire often enhances less than brilliant brushwork through a softening of edges, crystal development, or an unexpected richness and variety of color, but the fired tin glaze displays exactly what has been painted on it. Any weakness or hesitation in the stroke is clearly evident, whereas Alan's precisely rendered line retains all its clarity. Every nuance and subtlety is preserved and each stroke remains clearly identifiable even in the most complex compositions.

Since he feels very strongly about the importance of the integration of form and decoration in his pottery, and because even the word "decoration" seems to suggest something added rather than an integral part of the concept, Alan prefers to call his work "painted pottery." He feels the term implies a unified whole. The concept involves not only fitting the decoration to a given form, but designing the form itself with the decoration in mind. The forms are usually simple, with straight or gently curved surfaces, to accommodate the brushwork. A given form, however, may be painted in many different, but equally valid ways.

Traditionally, most tin-glazed earthenware has been produced by a collaboration of potter and painter, sometimes resulting in a lack of real integration of form and decoration. The painting was often regarded as more important than the form, and in extreme

Alan:
Ideally, each pot should be shaped with at least a general idea of how it will be painted, and the painting should be done with an appreciation of the form as a whole. For the painting is not just a decorative finish: it is an inseparable part of the completed object. By alternating between throwing and painting, a potter comes to appreciate these two processes as complementary to each other, not as separate operations.

examples decoration was imposed on the pot with complete disregard of the form. To avoid this kind of dichotomy, everyone at Aldermaston does both throwing and painting and almost always decorates the pieces he himself has thrown.

The initials on the bottom of each pot are "A" for Aldermaston coupled with the surname initial of the painter, who in most cases was also the thrower.

COMMISSIONS

Partially because the majolica technique seems amenable and partially because he enjoys collaborative projects, Alan is receptive to many types of special requests and ideas proposed by customers, which many contemporary potters would avoid. He does not accept everything, of course, but has often made things he would never have thought of himself, even some which he disliked the idea of at first. He finds commission work exciting and challenging, forcing him to work with new ideas, often with results that are surprising even to himself and some that initiate a growth and development in his work as a whole.

Most commissions are for variations of the normal work, involving more or less standard forms, such as dinner sets or goblets with special decoration, or party or special occasion pieces such as large plates, punch bowls, or large jugs. Commemorative inscriptions are often requested, which Alan's skill as a calligrapher enables him to execute brilliantly, incorporating the lettering into the overall design. Some commissions, however, present a greater challenge, forcing Alan to search for solutions to problems he has not previously confronted, such as a recent project for a church: a series of large tiles depicting the stations of the cross. Much of the commission work is done entirely by Alan or Edgar, but some of the more routine, less demanding orders are handled by the other potters, and a few pieces are made by them and painted by Alan.

Alan:
I like doing commission work. The whole process is exciting and satisfying. Usually somebody has an idea which he has only half seen in his mind and has to try to communicate it to me. Then I have to decide if I can do it, and of course it is clear that I am not going to do exactly what he thought of in the beginning. But if he can put the seed of his idea into my mind, it will be interpreted and transformed, and the outcome will be a marriage of two people's ideas. Frequently a customer's ideas break into my own set ideas with a most constructive and stimulating effect. A great many things that I have learned have resulted from following up commissions, about which I may have felt diffident in the beginning.

Two standard casserole forms, with the same decorative pattern, but with variations in spacing, details, and execution.

Goblets with varying styles of decoration. The one on the right is painted in yellow lustre, the others in majolica colors.

Standard ware, covered dish with painting in brown, gray, and green, 10" (25.4 cm) high.

29

MICHAEL AND SHEILA CASSON

Wobage Farm

UPTON BISHOP, HEREFORDSHIRE, ENGLAND

Left
Mick and Sheila attaching handles, Prestwood.

Right
Large storage jar by Mick, poured glaze.

For 30 years Michael Casson has been making pots, and for 18 years he and his wife Sheila operated a small pottery in the village of Prestwood, about 30 miles northwest of London in Buckinghamshire. Mick and Sheila work together, though each makes his own pots. They make a standard line of domestic stoneware as well as individual work in stoneware and porcelain. At Prestwood about one-third of the production was sold retail from the studio, while the rest was sold through galleries. In 1977 they moved to a new home and studio on a farm near Gloucester in Herefordshire. The move is not only a change to a new location and a more spacious workshop, but it also marks a change in their approach to their work. Mick and Sheila plan to do little or no direct selling to the public, make less standard repeat ware, and concentrate more on individual work.

In addition to being a production potter, Mick was an influential teacher for 20 years at the Harrow College of Art and was one of the founders, and for 12 years a member of the executive board of the Craftsmen Potters' Association, whose members include most of the best potters in England. The C.P.A., among other activities, operates a gallery/shop in London that sells the work of its members and publishes a bimonthly pottery journal, *Ceramics Review,* for which Mick has written a number of articles. He has also done a television series on pottery for the B.B.C., which became the basis for an excellent pottery guide published by the B.B.C. in 1977.

Warm, open, and enthusiastic, Mick enjoyed teaching and found the mutual stimulation of students and colleagues exciting. He also enjoys contacts and exchanges with other potters and often expresses intense admiration and feeling for the work of oth-

ers, although he seems little influenced by them in his own work, except in methods and techniques.

The Cassons thoroughly enjoy their work and approach it in a relaxed yet disciplined and methodical manner. Mick gave up teaching in 1973 to devote himself full time to his pottery and the income from their modest production has been sufficient for their simple yet comfortable way of life. They feel no pressure to produce more, or to concentrate on types of work that bring the greatest monetary return for time invested.

Mick and Sheila have three children (two daughters, 18 and 20, and a son, 11. All have worked with clay and learned to throw, but show no inclination to become potters.

BACKGROUND

Like many other potters, Michael Casson originally wanted to be a painter, and became involved with clay by chance. He first studied pottery just after World War II, during an 18-month emergency training course for teachers, which required him to study a craft as well as drawing and painting. After two years of teaching, he returned to school (Hornsey School of Art), still intending to be a painter, but changed over to pottery. In 1952, after three years of art school that gave him a wide awareness of art and design, but provided little technical, practical training (none in firing), he set up his own studio in London with the intention of making sculptural pieces and some pots. Although his work sold reasonably well, the pieces were time-consuming to make, and he depended on teaching for his livelihood.

During the next few years, however, Mick began to use more of his own and other people's pots in his home. His enjoyment in actually using pots led him to think more in terms of making practical functional ware, which at first took the form of brush-decorated tin-glazed earthenware. In 1955 he married Sheila, whom he had met at art school and who was also a potter. She began working with him, and together they gradually went through the process of teaching themselves the basics of production potting. Mick continued to make some sculptural pieces, but concentrated more and more on functional ware. Their ultimate goal was to earn a living as potters, and by 1958, Mick and Sheila felt that this was possible. With the idea of converting to the production of stoneware and selling a substantial portion of their work from their own showroom, they purchased a home and studio in the village of Prestwood. This location was close enough to London for easy access to galleries and Mick's part-time teaching job so a gradual transition could be made. Shortly after the move, however, Mick became involved in planning a new pottery course at the Harrow College of Art and continued there as a teacher until 1973.

TEACHING

While living in London, Mick taught pottery courses at several schools on a part-time basis, at one time teaching four evenings a week as well as Saturday mornings, so he could save enough money to get a better studio.

His most significant teaching experience, both in terms of his influence as a teacher and his personal development as a potter, was at the Harrow College of Art. Although since 1973 he has devoted himself entirely to his own pottery, he still speaks in glow-

Exterior of the barn-studio, Wobage Farm.

The 16th-century house at Wobage Farm.

Mick:
My work sold, but I couldn't earn a living at it. There wasn't a big market for functional ware. I wasn't good enough to produce it anyway, and my intentions were muddled. Of course Bernard Leach, his sons, followers, and a few others were there, very definitely knowing what they were doing, pursuing Leach's idea of making functional pots for a living. I read Leach's A Potter's Book about 1949, and although I recognized it as a great book and a marvelous philosophy, it didn't mean that much to my work at that time. I was involved in sculptural pieces, and if I made tableware, it was done very slowly, very laboriously; my throwing was awful.

ing terms of his Harrow experience. Mick, along with Victor Margrie, the head of the pottery department at Harrow, developed a new studio pottery workshop course in 1963. They could see the growing market for functional domestic tableware and the rapidly improving prospects for making a living as a potter. However, they felt that art school courses generally did not offer the kind of practical training that would prepare a student to become a professional potter. They designed an intensive two-year course that concentrated on production throwing and a sound technical foundation.

There were only a few students at first, but the course was soon drawing students from Australia, New Zealand, and America as well as from England and other European countries. No more than 16 new students were accepted each year, although in 1973 there were more than 100 applications. While Mick was at Harrow, about 110 students completed the two-year course, 75 percent of whom became professional potters, most with their own studios.

Mick enjoyed teaching, but after ten years of intense involvement in the Harrow course (the last two years as head of the department) he felt the need to spend more time on his own work. During those years the increased skill and efficiency he had developed in his potting made him more confident of his ability to make a good living solely as a potter (which had always been his ultimate goal).

Mick:
In those two years we taught them the fundamentals of making a narrow chunk of pottery—domestic tableware. We started with clay bodies, glazes, throwing, how to make a wheel, how to build kilns, and how to make a living at making pots. It was a time of great ferment for me. We had mostly highly motivated students in their mid-twenties and a staff who were all professional potters, and so many things happened: the exchange of ideas, the techniques that came out of it! It was very exciting! For me personally, my technique was improved, my speed was doubled within a year, my thinking was radically altered.

STUDIO AND EQUIPMENT

The small Prestwood pottery was well organized and workable within the limitations imposed by the buildings themselves, but had for years been bulging at the seams. The spacious new studio at Wobage Farm, though accommodated in existing buildings and subject to arbitrary size restrictions, is a model of logical planning and efficient use of space.

Prestwood. The Cassons' trim red brick home and studio in Prestwood had formerly been a greengrocer's shop with living quarters behind and above. This arrangement was retained, with the throwing room and display area occupying the wide but shallow former shop, while clay preparation and glazing areas and the kilns were in a separate building behind the house. Large show

Street front of the Prestwood studio.

Mick throwing a bowl,
Prestwood.

windows on the street front were used for displaying pots and, though partially curtained to separate display and work areas, they also gave passersby a view of Mick and Sheila at work. The white-painted, wood-paneled studio walls were lined with open shelves holding pots, bats, buckets of slip, and tools, while more tools were hung on the wall. There were two Leach-type treadle wheels, a wedging table, work tables, and a large sink. Though relatively small, the room had a spacious feeling because of its simplicity, uncluttered organization, white walls, and large windows.

Except for a narrow side room used for storage of prepared clay, the rest of the building was living quarters. Small and cramped when the Cassons came in 1958, the living space was enlarged by an addition built in 1966. The first floor contained the kitchen and living-dining room with large windows opening onto a secluded garden, while bedrooms and an office were on the second floor.

The glazing area and the gas and electric kilns were in a one-story brick building behind the house. Attached to the back of this building was a partially enclosed shed, providing shelter for a large clay mixer and a wood-fired kiln and its fuel supply.

Wobage Farm. After resigning his teaching position in 1973 to devote himself full time to potting, Mick began to think seriously about moving to a more spacious studio. Since it was no longer crucial to be near London, and property within commuting distance of the city had become very expensive anyway, Mick and Sheila finally decided on Wobage Farm, three-and-one-half acres on Crow Hill near Upton Bishop in Herefordshire. Worthy of its picturesque name, Wobage Farm is a 16th-century farmhouse with half-timber front and three magnificent old stone and brick barns that stand on an open hill overlooking a wide landscape of pastures, fields, and forest. Because of the unspoiled rural setting and the historic character of the buildings, the county government was concerned about how they would be used. Fearing the studio might grow into a factory, the county granted permission for it with the provisions that the Cassons live in the house and that no more than 1500 sq. ft. of the 8000 sq. ft. total area of the barns be used for pottery making. Additional space may be used for kilns, storage, or other crafts, but the same space limitation applies for each craft. Sheila's father, a woodworker, will live with them and use part of the one barn for his own workshop. Mick envisions the possibility of having other craftsmen working there as well, including his daughters, who are planning to work in textiles.

The barns, which until a year ago were used as cowsheds, required a great deal of work, and the house also needed wiring, plumbing, and extensive repairs. One barn has been converted for studio use with the installation of plumbing, heating, electricity, and concrete floors. The massive stone and brick exterior is unaltered except for the addition of large windows, sensitively proportioned and placed to avoid disrupting the character of the structure. A long, narrow one-story wing houses the throwing, glazing, and kiln rooms. An adjoining 30 ft. x 40 ft. (9.1 m x 12.3 m) two-story section contains a clay preparation and storage room and the woodworking shop on the ground floor; a textile studio is planned for the second floor. A wood-fired kiln, wood storage, and dry-materials storage are in the other barns. The new studio is superbly functional, while preserving the rustic beauty

The glaze room, Wobage Farm studio.

The throwing room, Wobage Farm studio.

Top
Squared storage jar (thrown and altered) by Mick, orange ash glaze, 8″ (20.3 cm) diameter.

Above
Pitcher by Mick with combed decoration.

The 50-cu.-ft. downdraft oil-fired kiln (far left) and the 25-cu.-ft. wood-fired kiln for salt firing (left), Wobage Farm.

Right
Storage jar by Mick.

of the barn in whitewashed stone walls, and exposed beams and rafters. Compact yet spacious, there are clearly defined, logically organized areas for throwing, glazing, clay preparation, etc., and carefully planned shelving and storage space.

Kilns. At Prestwood, pots were usually bisque-fired in a small electric kiln (although the gas kiln was sometimes used) to about 950°C, judging by eye. Glazed ware was reduction-fired to about 1280°C in the 22-cu.-ft. natural gas downdraft kiln that Mick built in 1963. A glaze firing proceeded rapidly up to 1000°C when reduction was begun (heaviest between 1100°C and 1180°C), continuing to near the end of the 14-to-15-hour cycle, which was completed with a 20-to-30-minute oxidation period. There was a temperature variation of about 40°C (1260°C—Seger cone 8—at the top to about 1300°C at the bottom), which Mick found convenient for the varying maturing points of his glazes. A recently built wood kiln was fired only a few times before being dismantled in preparation for the move to the new studio.

At Wobage Farm Mick has built two kilns: a 50-cu.-ft. spring arch downdraft kiln-fired with two oil burners and used for both bisque and glaze firing, and a 25-cu.-ft. wood-fired-kiln that will be used for salt firing. The oil kiln and a small electric kiln are in the kiln room adjoining the glazing area, while the wood kiln is in a separate shed.

ASSISTANTS

During most of his Harrow years Mick actually taught classes at the school only one day a week, but was involved with the program and the students in other ways as well. The course included workshop experience in the studios of the teachers, so that there was often a student working with him for two or three weeks.

Mick employed some of his former Harrow students as throwing assistants for short periods, and for about six months, two of

Variations on a theme: massive storage jars by Mick with both sgrafitto and inlaid slip decoration.

them at once. They were both very fast repetition throwers and threw standard tableware forms designed by Mick. Their production was so great that Mick, who made handles for some pieces and did all of the decorating and glazing as well as loading and firing the kilns, had little time for making his own pots.

Mick does not intend to hire apprentices or throwing assistants in the future, but has considered the possibility of another kind of employee.

WORK CYCLES

Mick and Sheila normally work six days a week from about 9 A.M. to 6 P.M. and occasionally work after dinner and on Sundays.

Because they work alone, a cyclical rhythm seems most logical. At Prestwood the cycle was about one month, with three weeks devoted to making pots. Usually there were two bisque firings in the electric kiln every weekend (taking advantage of a lower weekend rate for electricity). When enough pots had accumulated for two or three glaze firings in the 22-cu.-ft. gas kiln, they moved into the back studio for the glazing cycle. Mick and Sheila use the same glazes, but each normally glazes and decorates his own work. Since the kiln was small and glazing and decorating are generally done simply and quickly, enough pots could be glazed and the kiln packed within two days. It was fired on the third day, and by the time it was cool enough to unload, a second group of pots was ready to go in.

In planning the new studio, Mick did not want a very large kiln that would force him into a long work cycle. He likes to see finished pots fairly often, as well as glaze and body tests that are included in almost every firing. He felt that the ideal size to accommodate the scale of his production on a schedule that suited his temperament would be about twice as big as the Prestwood kiln. Accordingly the first kiln he built at the new studio has a 50-cu.-ft. capacity that will hold about two or three weeks' work in a single glaze firing.

SALES

When the Cassons moved to Prestwood in 1959, it was with the idea of selling a substantial portion of their work through the studio shop to local residents. In recent years about one-third of the production was sold in this way (mostly standard tableware such as mugs, small bowls, pitchers, and teapots), while most of the larger, more expensive and more individual pieces were sold through galleries. Although in recent years an increasing number of customers came from London, most of the sales at the studio were to residents, many returning regularly and often. Mick and Sheila felt an obligation to continue their original idea of supplying functional ware to the people around them. Toward the end, however, they began opening the shop only one day a week, after years of being open daily. In their new studio, located in a more remote and thinly populated area, they will not have a retail shop at all, but plan to sell all their work through five galleries: three in London (the Craftsmen Potters' Association, the British Crafts Center, and the Casson Gallery, owned by Mick's sister) and one in Dartington and one in Surrey.

Demand for the Cassons' work is high, relative to their modest production, and the pots consistently sell very quickly. There is rarely a large selection of finished pots at the studio except just after a firing. Galleries are happy to buy whatever Mick makes, and some even have waiting lists for some types of pots. Mick never seems to be far enough ahead of current demand to regularly set aside special pieces in anticipation of possible exhibitions, but he does save outstanding pieces when he knows a show is scheduled (usually a year or more in advance). Mick has had virtually no problems with compromising what he really wanted to make and what would sell.

Pricing. In the early 1960s Mick and the other potter-teachers at Harrow, as well as their students, systematically analyzed their work in terms of time, materials, and kiln space required for each type of pot relative to its market value. They did this not only as a means of arriving at modest and appropriate prices, but as part of an attempt to find ways of increasing their productivity. Despite some criticism that they were doing a disservice to art in applying business methods to artistic production, they felt that a potter could be financially independent only through efficient management of his resources and abilities. This kind of analysis, which contributed to Mick's increased speed and efficiency during that time, is no longer consciously part of his thinking except as a pricing guide.

Pricing of individual pots is based on a balancing of several factors, including size, amount of time required, and relative quality. Mick and Sheila always do the pricing together immediately after each firing. First they take out the seconds and "subs" that will be priced lower. Mick considers a second an otherwise good pot with a technical flaw (a crack, a bad warp, etc.), while a "sub" is technically all right but just hasn't come off esthetically. Then there are the good pots and one or two "racers" (a Harrow word for pieces that have come out exceptionally well technically and esthetically). These are priced somewhat higher, though never more than twice normal price. Standard production pieces have standard prices that remain constant, except for increases due to inflation. Individual pieces, made in shorter series, vary more and are relatively higher priced.

Mick only occasionally accepts orders or commissions, and then reluctantly, since he feels he does not do his best work under those conditions. In addition there is always a possibility of misunderstanding and dissatisfaction that doesn't occur when customers make their selections from among already-finished pots.

ANALYSIS OF WORK

The Cassons make a standard line of functional domestic stoneware as well as individual pieces in stoneware and porcelain. Generally they both make functional pots almost exclusively and use the same clay bodies and glazes and fire their work together in the same kilns. However, they make, decorate, and glaze their own work, and their styles are distinctly different.

Their standard repeat ware, which has been made largely for sale at the studio, includes mugs, cups and saucers, bowls, teapots, coffee jugs, pitchers, covered jars, casseroles, and other domestic ware (but rarely plates). The glazes, decoration, and many of the forms have remained essentially unchanged for several years to provide a continuity that would enable customers to gradually build up a group of coordinated tableware. Most of the smaller pieces and all the mugs are made by Sheila, who also does

Small porcelain bowl by Sheila.

Pedestaled bowl by Mick, incised landscape inlaid with white slip.

43

Storage jar by Mick.

a variety of larger pieces and especially enjoys making teapots and casseroles.

Mick tends to concentrate on larger pieces, such as bread crocks, storage jars, pitchers, jugs, and big bowls, but also relishes the special challenge of teapots. Mick's forms tend to be more vigorous and dramatic, while Sheila's are quieter, more sedate. Despite obvious differences, however, there is an affinity, partially due to the common glazes and firing, that makes their standard ware compatible and comfortable together. At Prestwood about 75 percent of Sheila's work was standard ware, while up to 75 percent of Mick's consisted of individual pieces, although the line between his repeat work and individual work is not sharply defined. In her individual work, Sheila moves in a completely different direction and has recently become involved in making small, delicate, precisely finished, sculptural bowl and vase forms.

Mick's pots are never spectacular in an obvious way. The forms are strong but simple, the glazes earthy and subtle, the decoration natural and unpretentious; but there is a potent, compelling quality in the larger storage jars and pitchers that approaches an archetypal dignity and presence. The pots are made with a vigor and excitement that gives them a warm, lively feeling despite their sometimes ponderous size, and a forcefulness and conviction that gives even his smaller pieces an imposing yet unpretentious monumentality. Mick handles clay easily, naturally, and vigorously and revels in the physical experience of throwing large pots. He throws quickly and forcefully, but with careful attention to the profile. Pots that are meant to be handled, such as teapots or coffee jugs, are pleasingly light and well balanced. Big pots tend to

Mick:
I enjoy making short runs of domestic stoneware, as I find the discipline a challenge. The forms have stayed basically the same for some years, although I attempt to modify and, I hope, improve their execution.

44

Bowl by Mick with brush decoration.

Bowl by Mick with landscape theme brush decoration.

Mick:
Function is very important to me, my pots are all usable. I take great care to make them function properly, and I feel they should be used. The form of a teapot is based on its specific function. I take immense trouble to position the spout properly, to be sure it pours well, that the handle is balanced, and all the rest. Casseroles that have a special body to withstand thermal shock should be used for cooking. The very big pitchers, I must admit, I see as vases with handles. I like people to put huge displays in them—big leaves or branches. People have used them for beer—that's great.

Above
Teapot with pulled handle and simple brush decoration in iron red on oatmeal glaze.

Large pitcher by Mick. The decorative patterns were made by quickly wiping with a sponge across a coating of wet slip.

be fairly heavy, but no more than is appropriate for their size and character. Details such as rims, spouts, handles, lugs, and knobs are deftly finished. Never fussy and never perfunctory, they always have a strong, definite, uncompromising boldness that matches the quality of the throwing.

Decoration. Mick prefers fast, direct methods of decorating, feeling that his work loses spontaneity and life with slower, more meticulous processes. His decoration is often minimal: a splash of poured glaze; casual patterns made with fingers, a sponge, or a wooden tool in wet slip; a few deft brushstrokes in iron red; or lightly incised banding accenting a shoulder or rim. His distinctive manner of attaching handles is often elaborated as a decorative element or accented by sweeping thumbnail incisions. Many pots are decorated in a more planned and deliberate manner, though still quickly executed and retaining a bold simplicity and strength appropriate to the forms. Motifs have often been derived from the idea of landscape, with stylized hills, fields, and trees appearing in many more or less obvious permutations, though they sometimes almost disappear in abstract designs or survive in undulating line patterns. The landscape theme has been developed in a variety of techniques, including brushwork, wax resist, sgraffito, incised lines, inlaid slip, paper resist, and applied clay. Though often painterly and pictorial in concept, the landscapes always remain schematic enough to function as decoration and are closely related to the forms.

Mick:
Form in a sculptural sense is my main interest, and any decoration I do comes from the form. The added pieces are themselves cut from thrown clay so that they will marry well with the thrown form.

Despite his preference for fast techniques Mick has achieved some especially beautiful results with the more painstaking processes of paper resist and mishima, or inlaid slip. For paper resist Mick uses thin soft paper such as newsprint to mask or stop out areas of the pot's surface while a slip coating is applied. The cut or torn paper shapes are first soaked in water, then arranged on the leather-hard pot, to which they readily adhere. After the slip has stiffened, the paper is peeled off. In the mishima technique, Mick uses thick white porcelain slip to fill a pattern of incised lines in a dark body. After the slip has stiffened, the pattern is cleaned up by lightly scraping the surface, leaving slip only in the incised lines.

Sheila's functional ware is usually simply glazed with brush decoration over the glaze. Some of her standard repeat pots are decorated by Mick. Her small porcelain pieces have delicate sculptural additions or precise carving and smooth, pale semiopaque glazes that accent the pristine quality of the material. Color decoration is limited to an occasional subtle blush of pink from a dip of copper slip under the glaze.

Function. Nearly all of the Cassons' pots are intended for use and functional considerations are important in designing and making each piece. Lids fit closely and solidly, spouts pour cleanly and handles, lugs, and knobs are a pleasure to hold as well as see.

Mick believes that medium and esthetic are inseparable, and his work, since his switch from earthenware, has been closely based on his vision of the particular qualities and strengths of reduction-fired stoneware. This is evident not only in his use of rich, earthy colors and textures of glazed and unglazed surfaces, but in strong, vigorous forms and decoration. His work has changed gradually over the years, gaining in assurance and mastery, while remaining true to his basic values. He is excited about

trying new glazes and techniques, but they are always assimilated into his steady line of development. Mick has in recent years done some porcelain, and these pieces have a lighter, more delicate character appropriate to the material, but still retain some of the sturdy, robust quality of his stoneware.

Mick and Sheila always make pots in groups or series. The more individual work is made in smaller groups, but they never attempt to make unique exhibition pieces, feeling that their best pots emerge from a natural rhythm of repetition. Each piece in a series is a variation of a single idea, but still important in itself and lively in concept and execution.

For Mick and Sheila the move to Wobage Farm is linked with a deliberate change in emphasis and direction in their work. This does not mean a sharp break with their past work, but a greater concentration on exploring their current interests and experimenting and developing new glazes, techniques, and ideas. They will make a greater proportion of larger, or more time-consuming, and therefore more expensive pieces, and less of the standard repeat ware.

Sheila:
When we had a shop, I made all the small domestic ware, and public demand made me spend most of my time making this. I started working in porcelain two years ago when I felt a need to do some more imaginative work. Now I feel I can stop making mugs, make fewer repeat items, and spend more time doing individual pieces in porcelain.

Mick:
I plan now to make pots in short series, maybe no more than half a dozen similar pieces at a time so I can explore various aspects in greater depth: functional things like handles, lids, and lips as well as decoration processes, whether that means inlaying clay or glaze, or wood-firing porcelain in a salt atmosphere to achieve a certain color and surface effect. It was to get involved in the type of work that needs more space with different kilns, little or no direct selling to the public, that we moved to Herefordshire.

Top left
Standard mugs with wax-resist decoration made by Sheila.

Left
Pedestaled bowl by Mick, incised landscape inlaid with white slip.

Right
Pitcher by Mick with dark red body, poured ash, and tenmoku glazes, 13″ (33 cm) high.

KARL CHRISTIANSEN

The Pot Shop
WILTON, IOWA

Left
Karl throwing a large plate on the electric wheel.

Right
Saki bottle, thrown and altered form with separate filling and pouring spouts, decorated in white, red, and black glazes, and iron oxide brushwork.

Karl:
I have learned to love living in Iowa. I like the farmland and the farmers and the river; and this small town is a delight. Iowa City, with the University and all it has to offer, is not far away. I feel settling here in Wilton was good fortune, as the town and this area have satisfied my needs very well.

Karl Christiansen decided to become a potter in 1963 after five years of teaching high school and college art. In 1966 he established his present studio in Wilton, Iowa. His modest production, all wheel-thrown reduction-fired stoneware, is sold mostly at art fairs, with a small proportion sold at the studio or through galleries and shops. Since 1972 Karl has been assisted by a series of apprentices, but they have not participated in making his pots.

Karl began as a potter with the idea of supplementing his sales income with part-time teaching, and for ten years taught pottery classes one day a week at a municipal art center in Davenport, Iowa. Although he enjoyed teaching, he resigned in 1975 because of irreconcilable differences with a new director. It meant losing a dependable regular income, but it also meant simplifying his life and gaining a day and evening. Karl's production has increased, but not enough to compensate for the lost teaching income. Nevertheless, he feels it has not necessitated any change in lifestyle. Karl has also taught pottery three times during summer session at the University of Iowa, and normally conducts two or three workshops per year, mostly at Iowa colleges.

Located at the edge of Wilton, a small town surrounded by rich farmland, Karl's studio and home are located on a five-acre plot with cornfields on two sides. He enjoys the relaxed pace of small-town life and does not feel isolated.

The Christiansen family life, though logistically complex, runs smoothly and amicably. Karl and his first wife Shirley had six children. In 1971 they were divorced and Karl married his present wife, Mary, who also had six children. Shirley and Mary's former husband were also married and live about 175 miles away. The twelve children, aged 10 to 23, are divided about evenly, although there is considerable movement between the two households, and at a given time there could be from two to ten children present. Each member of the family has his own schedule and activities, but normally all get together for dinner at six o'clock. Several of the children, especially the boys, have sometimes helped Karl in the studio or at art fairs, but only his oldest son, Karl Jr., has maintained a continued interest and is now earning part of his living through making pottery. Karl envisions the possibility of his son eventually returning to work with him and perhaps carrying on the studio after him.

Both Shirley and Mary, in addition to running the household and giving moral support, have helped with the pottery business in numerous ways, including keeping the books, figuring taxes, pricing and packing pots, making deliveries, and dealing with customers at the studio and at art fairs. In addition they have assisted with studio jobs such as mixing glazes, unloading clay deliveries, and waxing and sanding bottoms of pots. Mary also makes macramé hangers for Karl's planters.

Karl has a 22-ft. sailboat and enjoys sailing with Mary or one of the children on the Mississippi River or on Lake Michigan, where his parents have a summer home. He sometimes prefers to sail alone, as he did in the summer of 1977, when he made a ten-day, 250-mile trip, crossing Lake Michigan twice. He enjoys the solitude, the silence, the challenge, the elimination of extraneous matters, and the simplicity of sailing alone. When he can afford a larger, properly fitted boat, he would like to sail the Atlantic.

Karl:
I owe a great deal to Shirley and Mary, who have each made enormous and basically invisible or unrecognized contributions to my success as a maker of pots. I am fortunate to have had the support that these two strong women have given me in my rather self-centered drive to do what I wanted with my life.

BACKGROUND

Although he studied and taught art for years, Karl did not become involved in pottery until he was 28. He grew up in Minnesota and earned a B.A. in art at Concordia College. During the next two years spent in the army, he decided to become an architect. Soon after entering architectural school at the University of Minnesota, however, he realized that it was not a realistic goal, and transferred to the graduate school, where he earned an M.A. in art education in 1956. He taught high school art in Minnesota for two years, then was offered a position at Luther College in northern Iowa. During his first year there, he was asked to add ceramics to his teaching repertoire, and for that reason enrolled the following summer in his first pottery class at the University of Iowa. He was immediately caught up in the excitement of throwing, and returned reluctantly to Luther in the fall after an exhilarating summer of involvement in pottery. To continue his study, for the following year he was granted a leave of absence, which was extended to two years. During the second year he began seriously to consider the idea of becoming a full-time professional potter.

After earning an M.F.A. in ceramics at Iowa, Karl taught for one more year at Luther. During this time he decided to try to make a living as a potter while doing some part-time teaching, at least in the beginning. He found the kind of teaching situation he wanted at the Davenport Art Center, which was just initiating a pottery

Karl:
We devoured Leach's A Potter's Book; *it had a real impact on me, but the possibility of emulating his example seemed romantic, remote, impractical at first. Two of my teachers at the University of Iowa were important influences in my decision to become a potter. Carl Fracassini gave me reason for doing it, but it was Jim McKinnell who taught me how to do it. He was the catalyst. Through his example of actually having made a living as a potter at a time when very few were doing it, and in teaching us how to build an inexpensive kiln that could be easily dismantled, altered or moved, he opened up the possibility of going out and getting started with limited resources.*

Above
Hanging planter with incised
and pierced decoration, and
sculptural lugs.

Teapot with overlapping white,
iron red, and black glazes, and
brushwork in iron oxide.

Exterior of the studio with the original garage (foreground), tall barn (background), connected by the new addition (center).

Loading the first bisque firing in the new kiln.

program, and in the fall of 1963, he moved with his wife and children to Davenport.

Since his teaching job would not begin for several months and he did not yet have a studio, Karl found temporary employment in a small venetian blind factory. The owner, Ray Taylor, provided space and an interest-free loan to enable him to set up a studio in the factory. It was not a highly productive period for Karl, but it was a beginning, and the arrangement was continued for about nine months.

Karl's next studio was on a farm near Davenport, where the owner, Chris Tracy, provided space in a barn in exchange for his choice of one pot from each firing. The barn, which also housed his own metal and woodworking shop, had been renovated and had heat, electricity, and running water. Karl worked alone there for about four months before being joined by Carl Sande, who had been a fellow student at Iowa.

Sande, too, was dissatisfied with teaching and was anxious to try to make a living as a potter. The working relationship they developed continued until 1971, when Sande left to set up his own studio. They were never partners; finances were separate, and Sande simply paid a fixed amount per month for supplies and gas for the kiln. They shared the jobs of clay and glaze preparation, kiln loading, firing, and studio maintenance. Each made his own individual pots, but they used the same clay and glazes, normally fired together, and often exhibited and sold together. Karl feels that he learned a great deal from Sande, but although they shared many attitudes and ideas about pottery and inevitably influenced each other, their pots remained distinctly different.

Karl:
Once I had decided to try pottery, I can't remember ever feeling that I would fail at it, and have to go back to something else to make a living.

By 1966 Karl had decided to try to find a place of his own that could be both home and studio. Since he was teaching one day a week in Davenport, he looked for a place near there, and eventually bought a five-acre plot with house, garage, and chicken house in Wilton, about 20 miles west of Davenport. Though somewhat shabby and neglected, the simple Victorian house was sound and functional, and was eventually converted by the Christiansens into a warm, comfortable home with a spacious living room that opened onto a screened porch facing the studio.

Karl and Carl Sande continued to make pots at Tracy's farm while preparing the new studio. They insulated and lined the interior of the garage, installed a heating stove and shelving, and gradually moved the studio equipment from the farm. The kiln shed had been designed to be moved intact, and it was attached to the back of the garage studio. Finally the kiln itself was dismantled and rebuilt at the new site.

STUDIO AND EQUIPMENT

The original converted garage is still the core of the studio, but later additions have greatly expanded the space. In 1970 the chicken house was replaced by a tall barn with large high windows. This was used as a wood and metal shop and was equipped with power tools and welding equipment. It also served as a private studio for apprentices. As the 10-ft. high interior of the barn proved expensive to heat and additional storage space was needed, a floor was installed to make a second story in 1975. In 1976 Karl dismantled the kiln shed and replaced it with a larger structure connecting the main studio and the barn. This addition houses the glazing area and a separate room for the apprentice as

Casserole with tan and brown glazes.

Coffee jug with matt white and celadon glazes, brush decoration in iron oxide and rutile.

well as the kiln room. Karl has built steel-frame ware carts to make possible easy movement of pots between the different parts of the expanded studio. With the completion of the latest addition Karl, for the first time, made a careful analysis of his work habits. As a result, he attempted to reorganize spaces and movement patterns to eliminate inefficiency that resulted from the physical limitations of the studio itself, or from unnecessary movement of pots.

In 1963 Karl designed and built his own wood-frame kick wheel and built a few for other people as well. While Karl was working at Tracy's farm, Tracy, who was interested in mechanical things and whose wife was a pottery student, refined and improved the design and built a good but inexpensive wheel, which he continues to manufacture on a small scale. Of the three kick wheels in Karl's studio, one is an original prototype, while the other two are improved versions built by Tracy. Karl now does most throwing on a Shimpo electric wheel but uses a kick wheel for trimming and decorating.

Clay is prepared in 1000-pound batches, by mixing about 800 pounds of dry ingredients with an excess of water in a large stock tank. After the clay is allowed to slake for two or three days, the water is pumped off the top and the settled clay is put into large plaster drying bats that each hold about 80 pounds. When the clay has sufficiently stiffened, which may take from one to three days or longer, depending on temperature, humidity, and air movement, it is ready for wedging and immediate use. Karl finds this natural method produces a dense, smooth clay with throwing qualities superior to clay mixed by faster mechanical methods. The clay needs no further aging, and in fact Karl prefers to use it fresh.

Kilns. The simple 30-cu.-ft. downdraft insulating brick kiln that Karl used for almost all firing until 1976 was originally built at the venetian blind shop, and subsequently dismantled and rebuilt at Tracy's farm and at Wilton. It was dismantled a third time in 1976 and rebuilt as a 24-cu.-ft. car kiln. Fired with four forced-air burners built by Karl (each with its own small army surplus blower motor) that burn propane at about one-pound pressure, the kiln reaches cone 10 in about 12 hours.

The 1976 kiln room expansion plans also included an 80-cu.-ft. downdraft car kiln, which was not completed until 1978. The new kiln has unusually massive steel framing, and the sprung arch is supported by two arch-shaped trusses, functioning as large C-clamps, instead of the normal tie rods. It is fired with four high-pressure natural draft burners using propane at 10 pounds pressure. A cone 10 firing takes about 18 hours.

ASSISTANTS

Karl:
When Sande and I were here together we never considered apprentices because the shop was small and the two of us worked together. We had energy and enjoyed doing everything that needed to be done, but when he left I began to think about taking an apprentice. I have had numerous requests from young people wanting to come and work here, and I've always found people with some experience, who don't expect to be paid for their labor, but simply want use of space and materials in exchange for investing some of their own time in helping me.

During the years when Carl Sande was working with him, Karl never felt any need for an assistant, but since 1972 he has taken a succession of apprentices (five, including the present one), who have stayed for periods of from four months to two years.

Karl's first apprentice was a university pottery student who was looking for summer workshop experience. In exchange for instruction as well as materials, work space, and firing, he worked 20 hours a week for Karl, doing studio jobs, such as preparing clay and glazes, making plaster bats, and general cleaning and maintenance. He was not involved in making any of Karl's pots. In his free time he made his own pots with Karl's guidance and criticism. These were his to sell or keep and could be sold at the studio, but were kept separate from Karl's work.

Subsequent apprentices have all stayed for longer periods. One of them, Karl's sister Sonja, stayed for almost two years. The working arrangement with each apprentice has been essentially the same as with the first one. The agreements have been verbal and open-ended regarding the length of time, and have included a provision allowing either Karl or the apprentice to terminate the relationship at any time without question.

Terri Butters, the current apprentice, is the first to do any work on Karl's pots. Her involvement has been minimal: waxing bottoms, rims, and lids of pots before glazing and applying inlaid glaze on some bisque pots with incised decoration. This simple, but time-consuming process involves brushing on glaze to fill the incisions, then scraping off the excess.

Terri is also the first apprentice with whom Karl has collaborated on pots, having decorated some small bowls made by her. He is considering the possibility of regularly producing some collaborative pots that would be marked with a studio stamp, while those he makes himself would continue to be signed. However, this is an area he is entering with caution.

Karl's former apprentices have had pottery experience before working with him and had ambition to become independent potters. All but one now have their own studios and are making a living partly or entirely through selling their work. During their time together, Karl has tried to help each one develop his own particular skills and ideas, and he has tried to avoid simply inculcating his own personal convictions.

Despite this admonition, however, Karl's influence has been very strong, and some of his former apprentices still make pots that are very similar to his.

Karl:
At first I wouldn't let the apprentice touch my pots. He didn't even load the kiln. I was so determined that my pots were mine and I was going to do absolutely everything with them. I've moved away from that a little bit now.

For me, having apprentices has been a good experience. I have gotten work from them, but I also got satisfaction by investing in them some of what I have as a teacher. I have sat down with all of them and looked at groups of pots and given critiques. But I emphasize that my criticism is based on my personal opinions. I have strong convictions and I tell them, "If you listen only to me, you will be convinced that my method is the method and you will tend to be a little carbon copy. Ultimately you have to determine for yourself what you believe is your path and your idea of what a good pot is."

Above
Three small vases with incised
(left) and brush (center)
decoration.

Vase form with brush
decoration.

Above
Hanging planter with incised
and pierced decoration, and
sculptural lugs.

One of Karl's art fair display
units utilizing pipe fittings and
old barn boards.

WORK CYCLES

The work pattern is definitely cyclical, with almost all pots fired in the cycle in which they were made. There is very little carryover of raw or bisque ware to the next cycle. Work cycles vary in length and are determined by deadlines for shows, art fairs, or wholesale commitments rather than personal preference or kiln capacity. The schedule is usually based on about one deadline per month, except in January and February when the pace is slower and there is more time for contemplation and experimentation.

In meeting a deadline, Karl makes a schedule for the work cycle preceding it, working backward from the date of the latest possible glaze firing, and determining where each bisque and glaze firing should fall. He also makes a list of the types of pots and numbers of each he intends to make, keeping in mind how the combinations of sizes and shapes will fit into the kiln. Details of the schedule are often altered as the cycle progresses, but it serves as a basic organizational guide.

A typical one-month cycle might begin with a week of making large complex pieces that require a long drying time, followed by three or four days of throwing a lot of small simple pieces. These are then bisque-fired while Karl moves on to medium-sized pots of various types, finishing with more small pieces. While these last pots are drying, Karl begins glazing the pieces from the first bisque firing, and as soon as the second bisque firing is finished, the first glaze firing is ready to load. The second glaze firing follows in a few days, and often this three-kiln sequence is fired in a week. This schedule will undoubtedly be simplified as Karl begins using the new kiln, which has three times the capacity of the old one. Fewer firings will be necessary, although Karl feels he will be encouraged to make more large pieces.

Karl:
Sometimes I hate making pots. There are days when I am flat broke in terms of any inspiration, any energy, but I know I must work to meet a deadline. What surprises me is that on those days when I am feeling drained, it's almost as if my hands take over and make fairly decent pots. Of course I would elect to make simple, undemanding things on those days. Sometimes when I look at those pots the next morning, I am amazed that I could have felt so down about working in the pottery, because the pots are not bad. They are not a reflection of a disgruntled worker. But I think that just comes from having done it so much.

SALES

Karl has from the beginning sold a large part of his work at art fairs, which now account for 80 percent of his sales. The other 20 percent is sold wholesale, on consignment to shops and galleries, or retail at his studio. At first there was a balance between art fair and gallery sales, followed by a brief period when Karl and Carl Sande, questioning the dignity of selling on the streets, concentrated on increasing shop and gallery sales, both wholesale and consignment. They sent pots to galleries and shops in Chicago, St. Louis, and New York, as well as others nearer home, but became disillusioned as consignment sales generally proved slow and resulted in some irretrievable losses.

At this time in the mid-1960s the art fair phenomenon was burgeoning; the number of fairs was multiplying, and sales at the best ones were substantially increasing each year. Karl went to many different fairs, discovering through trial and error which of them were not worth the time and effort and which were highly profitable. Three of the Chicago fairs, at which he still sells, soon became the backbone of his economy for the year. Each year, Karl now usually goes to ten fairs, all in the Midwest during the summer and fall. Three times he combined art fairs in Florida with winter vacation trips, but since he dislikes driving long distances, Kansas City (about 200 miles) is the most distant on his current itinerary.

Karl sells pots wholesale to galleries in Chicago and on consignment through art centers in Des Moines and Davenport,

Karl:
The remarkable thing is I have never really had to worry about selling pots. The only problem was producing them; finding the time to make enough pottery to make a living has been the crucial thing for me. Now I believe this may be changing because of the proliferation of potters in the last few years. With so many new young potters, many of them excellent, it is no longer possible to be assured of getting accepted into the best juried art fairs each year. A few years ago a craft-hungry public quickly bought up all my production, but today because of the greater abundance and variety of pottery available, it is becoming a bit more difficult to turn my production into money. But perhaps a worried potter becomes a better potter.

Teapot with pulled handle, brush decoration.

Iowa, and a small co-operative gallery in Davenport, of which he is a member. This gallery takes only 15 percent of sales, in addition to modest membership dues. Although he sells only a small amount there during the year, Karl has had a standing arrangement for the last ten years to hold an annual exhibition-sale of his work on a weekend in late November, which has been consistently very successful. For this event Karl pays for advertising (announcements to people on his mailing list) and other expenses, as well as the 15 percent gallery commission.

Karl has never had a formal studio showroom and has never tried to develop a retail business at the studio. There are always pots for sale on display shelving in the workshop and often in the house as well, but Karl does not want to be tied to a regular showroom schedule.

Very few people in Wilton are interested in buying pots, and most studio customers come from Davenport or Iowa City. However, there has been considerable local interest in seeing the pottery studio, especially in the first few years. Kindergarten classes, 4-H groups, Cub Scouts, Campfire Girls, book clubs, and garden clubs have all arranged to visit.

Pricing. Karl's prices for most small-to-medium functional pieces tend to be comparatively low, and even the most expensive, elaborately decorated large vases and planters are modestly priced, considering the time and care lavished on them. Prices are

Karl:
The quality is the fine tuning. If one in a group of similar pots is obviously a finer piece of work, if something magical has happened in the making or in the firing, I recognize and value that, and I might add 10 or 20 percent to its price. Some customers recognize that difference; others may be more attracted to a pot that for me does not have that magic— it's very subjective.

based on the type and size of the pot and the time involved in making it. Although there is no standard repeat ware, prices for a mug or a casserole of a certain size are consistently within a narrow range, but small adjustments are made for particularly outstanding pieces.

Sales have never been a problem for Karl. His production is small and he is never very far ahead of demand.

ANALYSIS OF WORK

Karl's pots are, more than most, a reflection of the potter: warm, gentle but strong, honest, unpretentious, basically serious but with frequent whimsical touches. The pots have an easy, natural character and warm, lush color, yet retain tension, crispness, and clarity that give them strength. They are not spontaneous in feeling but do have a lively, human quality, although they are precise in form and finish. Beneath Karl's quiet, casual manner, wry humor, and seemingly imperturbable serenity, there is deep conviction and an uncompromising commitment to excellence. He is modest to the point of self-deprecation, rarely satisfied with his achievements and is continually striving to improve his work.

Types of Pots. Karl's production, which is entirely reduction-fired stoneware, includes bowls, plates, platters, mugs, vases, bottles, jugs, pitchers, teapots, coffee pots, covered jars, casseroles, soup tureens, ladles, and planters. The pots are all wheel-thrown and all are made in series, but except for sets, there is considerable variety in each group, and each piece has a distinct individual quality. The simple graceful thrown forms are sometimes gently flattened, squared, lobed, fluted, or carved. Some pieces, such as

Karl:

I see myself as being blessed with very minimal creativity and inventiveness. What I have done over the years is work very hard, experimenting, with lots of awful pots and dismal failures, to get to a point where I am halfway pleased with what I do. Throwing isn't easy for me. I don't do it with spontaneity. It is a rigid, calculated exercise. I have had to work very hard just to stay credible as a potter.

Dinner plate, wax-resist decoration.

Teapot, cups, cream pitcher, and sugar bowl, iron red glaze with iron oxide decoration.

large vases or pedestaled tureens, are assembled from two or three thrown sections.

Karl makes many teapots and saki bottles, both complex forms with thrown spouts and pulled handles. Teapots are almost always full, round forms with graceful, clearly articulated spouts. Handles are most often the overhead type, but there are occasional, sometimes whimsical variations. The saki bottles vary considerably in size and shape. Most recently they have been fairly consistent in having the top of the thrown body closed with a decorative knob that sometimes functions as a handle, with additions of a loop handle, an offset funnel-shaped filling neck, and a very narrow pouring spout.

Casseroles are an important part of Karl's production, but he uses no special ovenware body. He had used a petalite body to eliminate cracking caused by the expansion and contraction of heating and cooling. When petalite was no longer available, he stopped making casseroles for about a year until he could develop an alternative. After considerable research and study, he decided to concentrate on making the form rather than the material more thermal shock-resistant by eliminating sharp curves and maintaining an even thickness. He now makes casseroles with gently rounded shapes and only a shallow trimmed foot ring, and has had no reported cracking problems.

Function. Karl is very concerned with how his pots perform their intended functions and feels that a thoughtfully made functional pot can be fully appreciated only through using it.

Function is the first consideration for Karl, and a formal or decorative concept must conform to the requirements of intended use. This attitude extends beyond such obvious attributes as handles that comfortably fit the hand, spouts that pour cleanly with-

Karl:
I am unaware of any conflict between what I want to make and what will sell. I enjoy so much making everything, including coffee mugs, and they all sell, even those nonsensical little saki bottles with the funnel out the side. No one drinks saki, but people respond to them. I indulge myself. I really enjoy filling a ware board with those forms, varying the shapes and relationships of the funnel, spout, and handles.

Wine bottle, thrown and lightly paddled into square form, with overlapping glazes, and brush decoration.

out dripping, and lids that fit precisely and solidly, to such details as appropriate texture and color of glazes for ease of cleaning and attractive appearance with food.

Glazes and Decoration. Karl regularly uses 15 different glazes, some in two or three color variations. Glazing is done by dipping and pouring. Many pots are undecorated and are simply glazed in one or two colors, with various gradations achieved by multiple dipping. On others Karl may use three glazes dipped or poured to create overlapping panels of contrasting and intermediate colors, often further enriched with brush decoration. Brushwork is done on the raw glaze and is informal and nonrepresentational, based on a few simple strokes with a Japanese brush, usually with iron oxide or rutile. Wax resist is often used on plates and bowls. Some large vases, bottles, and planters are decorated with incised linear patterns accented with piercing. After bisque firing, the incised lines are inlaid with glaze that after firing shows through a contrasting glaze covering the pot.

Karl takes great pleasure in his work, but feels that people (especially part-time potters) often have an idealized, romantic conception of a potter's life. He emphasizes that he does not exist in a continual creative euphoria, that there are times of frustration—even boredom.

Karl's work has developed and changed slowly over the years. A form or decorative idea may serve as the basis for many variations over a period of months or years, but when he begins to feel that he has exhausted an idea or has begun merely to repeat successful formulas, he feels the need to break away and explore new ideas. This is not a compulsive drive to constantly make something new, but a realization that to make the most of his potential he must continue to develop and grow, and to maintain interest and excitement in his own work.

Left
Pitcher and cups in brown-and-white glazes.

Karl decorating a teapot with brushwork over the raw glaze.

67

JOHN GLICK
Plum Tree Pottery
FARMINGTON, MICHIGAN

Left
The forms of these large storage jars are subtly distorted as they are decorated with incised and impressed patterns.

Right
Covered jar 1977, 10" (25.4 cm) high. Decoration is incised and impressed with a rolling stamp.

A professional potter since 1964, John Glick has operated the Plum Tree Pottery in the Detroit suburb of Farmington, Michigan since 1965. Most of his production is sold direct to retail customers from the studio showroom or at art fairs, but some is consigned to galleries. His studio has been essentially a one-man operation, although he has had a series of apprentices and assistants. He makes a wide variety of functional and decorative reduction-fired stoneware with continually changing and evolving forms and decoration. Precise, analytical, and methodical about the business and technical aspects of his work, he is imaginative, intuitive, and spontaneous in making and decorating pots. From the beginning he has persisted in making only what is stimulating and challenging to him, and has achieved high productivity and financial success without sacrificing artistic growth.

John's wife, Ruby, whom he met while they were both students at Wayne State University, does freelance graphic design work in a studio adjoining the pottery showroom and handles most of the pottery sales. They have two children, Margaret, 15, and Ian, 6.

John has written articles on studio management and utilization of waste heat from kilns and glass furnaces for *Studio Potter* magazine. For several years he has been working on a book about studio management.

He is frequently asked to conduct workshops, usually on college or university campuses. Of the 20-to-30 workshop invitations each year, he usually accepts no more than two or three in

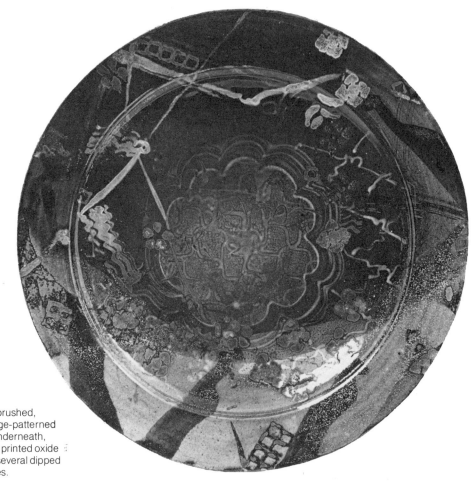

Large plate with brushed, trailed, and sponge-patterned slip decoration underneath, and brushed and printed oxide decoration over several dipped and poured glazes.

Large plate with sliptrailed and brush decoration on the wet pot, and calligraphic brushwork over multiple glazes.

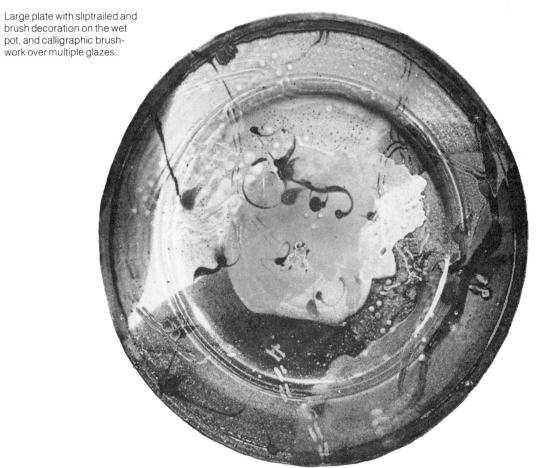

order to preserve a reasonably ordered life and work schedule. He has also taught two-or-three-week summer classes at Penland School of Crafts in North Carolina, Big Creek Pottery in California, and others. He devotes the same kind of careful planning, preparation, and intense personal involvement to his teaching as to his pottery.

BACKGROUND

John's interest in pottery began in high school, but at that time he did not consider becoming a potter. In fact, he began his studies at Wayne State University as a geology major. He soon realized, however, that his real interest lay in the arts, and he changed his major. Studying pottery with Bill Pitney, he developed a solid technical foundation and a thoughtful serious approach. In 1960, he earned a B.F.A. at Wayne State with a double major in ceramics and metalsmithing, and entered Cranbrook Academy with a scholarship in both ceramics and metalsmithing. After his first term there, he began to concentrate more and more on pottery. As a student, his dedication and voracious appetite for work were already evident in the long hours he devoted to potting and in finding places to work and to fire his large output during summer vacations.

His philosophy of continual exploration and development of ideas was formed at least partly through the influence of Maija Grotell, his ceramics teacher at Cranbrook. She stressed the importance of creative involvement in each piece, and the need for constant growth and development through evolving groups or series of forms, while discouraging high productivity achieved through mere repetition. Influenced by the example of potters Bernard Leach and Warren MacKenzie, whose work and philosophy he admired, John gradually decided that he wanted to be an independent studio potter.

In 1962 he received his M.F.A. from Cranbrook and in the same year was awarded a Tiffany Grant of $1,000 to help set up his own studio. This project was delayed until 1964, however, since he was drafted into the army soon after graduation. As a soldier he spent a year and a half in Germany near Höhr-Grenzhausen (a salt-glaze center since the 14th century) and was able to visit factories and studio potteries there.

When he returned to the Detroit area in 1964, John decided to rent space where he could set up a studio and try out the idea of making pottery for a living. Using hard fire brick dug out of the ground at an abandoned commercial kiln site, John built a 60 cu. ft. gas kiln that he fired 60 times in a year-and-a-half. During this period Ruby worked as an art teacher, which provided a steady income, but sales increased rapidly, and John was soon confident of his ability to make a living. In 1965, after a careful search for a permanent location, he bought a Victorian farmhouse with a garage and barn (now showroom and studio, respectively) on an acre of land near Farmington, Michigan. Although now nearly surrounded by the burgeoning development of suburban Detroit, John's immediate environment still retains some of its rural character. The name, Plum Tree Pottery, and the stylized leaf design used as a studio stamp (pressed into the bottom of each pot) and logo (used on stationery, postcards, sales receipts, and advertising) were inspired by the survivors of an old orchard next to the studio.

The present studio is the result of a gradual evolution and expansion over the last twelve years, although the original wide low-roofed barn remains the core. This building at first housed the kiln, bathtubs for clay mixing, and a small showroom as well as the work area. The studio has been rearranged and expanded several times as new equipment was added and the need for work, storage, and display space has grown. The original building contains about 1000 sq. ft. of floor space, while a kiln room addition provides 350 sq. ft. more. About one-third of the main building is occupied by a small office, a metal and woodworking shop, and a storage room for raw materials, while the remaining large space is divided by a center island of shelves and work tables. Eight large steel-frame ware carts facilitate movement of pots between work areas and the kiln room.

There are three wheels: one modified Soldner electric wheel and two heavy wood-frame treadle wheels patterned after the Leach wheel, but with improved bearings and linkage. The electric wheel is used for throwing small repeat pieces of from ½ to 10-pound size. For demanding or highly detailed pieces, John prefers the intimate control of the treadle wheels, which he also uses for trimming and decorating and for assembling composite forms.

The same stoneware body is used for most wheel and slab work. A large industrial type pug mill can process a three-month supply of clay (2500–3000 pounds) in one day. A commercial dough mixer, which had earlier replaced the bathtub for mixing clay, is still used for porcelain and ovenware bodies. Recent additions include a Brent slab roller, a Brent extruder used for making some handles and spouts, and a larger extruder built by John for making slabs of various configurations.

Part of the studio exterior. The tall building is the kiln room addition.

Kilns. John used a small gas Alpine kiln for the first few months in the new studio, until he completed a 40-cu.-ft. hard brick, catenary arch kiln. This was replaced in 1967 by a more efficient 60-cu.-ft. insulating brick kiln. However, by 1969, with the help of a throwing apprentice and a slab-building assistant, John's production had increased so much that a larger kiln was needed. Since he also needed more studio space, John decided to build an addition to house a new 10-cu.-ft. kiln. Completed in 1969 and still in use. this catenary arch, downdraft, walk-in kiln is built of insulating brick covered with a layer of insulating cement. The kiln is fired with two large forced-air burners that operate on low-pressure propane. A cone 10 reduction firing cycle of 25-to-30 hours provides the long-soaking firing that John feels is essential to achieve the kind of glaze quality and color development he wants. Safety shut-off equipment makes it possible for John to sleep during part of the firing, which is normally begun in the afternoon. Reduction is begun the next morning when the kiln has reached 1850° F and is continued to the end of the firing that evening.

A separate kiln shed, built in 1973, houses a small kiln used for supplementary bisque firing and a 30-cu.-ft. kiln designed for wood firing or for use as a sodium vapor kiln. To avoid the air pollution of salt firing, John substituted soda ash, which gives similar but less even glaze results. John experimented with vapor glazing until 1975, enjoying the irregular and unpredictable results, but in 1977 modified the kiln, which he now uses strictly for experiments in wood firing.

John's concern about dwindling oil and gas reserves has led

About half of the main work area is visible in this view.

John and Ruby unloading a glaze kiln.

him to explore alternative means of heating. The shop is now
heated by a small, highly efficient cast-iron wood stove, although
a gas furnace provides extra heat on exceptionally cold days. The
kiln room is not normally heated. He has recently installed a solar
collector on the roof that on sunny days will supply warm air to
the studio. In addition, he has also been trying to devise a system
for efficiently utilizing the heat lost from the kiln during firing and
cooling.

Showroom. The display and sales area was originally in a small
room in the studio building, and customers could watch John at
work and wander about the studio. At first John enjoyed this intimate contact with the customers, but as their numbers grew and
interruptions became more frequent, it became necessary to rope
off the display area from the studio. This somewhat awkward arrangement was eliminated and additional space was gained when
a large garage, formerly used for storage, was remodeled in 1971
to include a small studio for Ruby and a handsomely designed,
well-lighted showroom with built-in shelves. Ruby usually handles sales, although John still enjoys meeting customers when
time permits.

A large attic above the showroom is filled with shelves of finished pots, some of which are saved for John's own permanent
collection (comprised of several hundred pieces, including at least
one or two representatives of each form or decorative idea he has
developed over the years). Also set aside in the attic is a selection
of especially successful recent work from which pieces are chosen
for exhibitions.

John's ideal studio would be arranged more logically and conveniently than the space in the present buildings, but he feels
these things are not really important. The present studio is
spacious, well-equipped, and adaptable to changing needs, allowing him to work comfortably, efficiently, and productively.

ASSISTANTS

John did not have clearly developed ideas about apprenticing
when he set up the Plum Tree Pottery, but felt he would like to
work with other people. He had long admired the kind of workshop established by Bernard Leach at St. Ives, and was impressed
by his visits to several potteries in Germany where small groups
of people worked closely together. John has now worked with a

Slab-built boxes have been an important part of John's work for years. Usually formed in wood-press molds, boxes have ranged from simple to complex, convoluted, and compound shapes. Recently, John has been developing a series of boxes constructed of extruded slabs.

Left
Double box, 1972, 9" (23 cm) in diameter. Two semi-circular boxes together form a single entity. Decoration is clear and straightforward.

Right
Rectangular box, extruded slab construction, 1977, 13" (33.02 cm) long.

Left
Oval box, 1972, 10" (25.4 cm) X 13" (33.02 cm). Overlapping decoration of patterned slip, glazes, and oxide brushwork.

Right
A later, more complex shape with looser, overlapping decorative motifs.

series of apprentices in the studio for half of his 14 years as a professional potter. There have been seven, including the present
one, who worked in various capacities depending on their capabilities and what they and John hoped to achieve through their
relationship. The first apprentice stayed about a year, beginning
about six months after establishment of the pottery. She helped in
construction of slab pieces but did not throw. After another six
months of working alone, John started his second apprentice, Jan
Sadowski, who as a high school student began working after
school and on weekends. Later while attending college, he
worked only weekends and vacations. Jan had pottery experience
when he started and quickly developed into a highly skilled
thrower. He threw pots, for which John had developed prototypes, and he could duplicate John's forms consistently. John
sometimes altered and always decorated and glazed these pots.
Production was considerably increased, and there was virtually
no difference between pots made entirely by John and those made
cooperatively. He made a distinction, however, by signing the latter, while the others bore only the studio stamp. In addition to
throwing, Jan helped with clay and glaze preparation, kiln loading, the maintenance and cleaning of the studio, as well as assist-
ing at art fairs and was paid an hourly wage for studio jobs and a
piece rate for throwing. John enjoyed this highly productive relationship, but when Jan left he felt a need for a slower, quieter,
more contemplative interval of working alone, to develop more

new ideas and directions without the pressure of coordinating his work with that of an apprentice.

He worked alone for about a year. Then during the next four years he took four apprentices, three for just six months each, and one (subsidized by a Tiffany Grant) for a year. He felt that a long association, though rewarding in some ways, could be stifling for the apprentice. These assistants helped run the studio but did no production throwing. They made their own pots, learning from John, and a modest number of these were fired. Four years ago, as John began work on his book, his studio schedule became less regular. He did not take another apprentice until recently, preferring, for a time, the flexibility and privacy not possible with someone else in the studio.

For nine years, in addition to studio apprentices, John employed assistants who worked in their own homes assembling basic slab forms, using templates, wooden molds, and jigs. One assistant, a woman confined to a wheelchair, worked for John for two years; another, who left only recently, worked for seven years. Although they had no pottery experience, they were both adept with their hands and quickly learned the necessary skills. For each new form, John developed prototypes, then made the required templates, molds, and/or jigs and explained their use to the assistant in a brief training session. Prepared slabs were exchanged for assembled forms about three times a month. Through this system John was able to increase production, while retaining complete control of the product. It also enabled him to become personally involved in each piece, by adding handles, spouts or lids, detailing, and decoration, so each one became uniquely his.

Based on his varied experiences with apprentices, John has developed very definite ideas about how the working relationship should be structured to be most helpful in his own work, while also insuring meaningful artistic development as well as practical experience for the apprentice. Beth Mueller, who began working for him in 1977, is his present studio apprentice. He has established a three-part schedule with her that combines aspects of previous apprentice and assistant relationships. Beth is paid piece rate for throwing groups of small pots and for assembling basic slab forms, which are completed and decorated by John. She has a separate work space in the studio, and John plans the schedule to allow her time each day for her own work, in which she is directed by mutual agreement along specific avenues. They discuss her work in almost daily critiques, and perhaps 10 to 15 percent of it is saved and fired.

John:
I feel an obligation to make the apprenticeship experience rich in a variety of vital ways. An apprentice should become totally familiar with technical and skill-related aspects of pot-making, equipment, and studio lore, but should also gain a positive sense of self-development beyond practical training. I want to create a working arrangement that provides ample time for the apprentice's own individual work. We fire only a small amount of this work, but valuable experience is derived from making large series of related forms, and although breaking up some 90 percent of the pots is not easy, it helps to develop self-criticism and judgment. I do not believe in delegating any set of jobs to an apprentice. We work together on virtually all studio activities, such as cleanup, preparing clay and glazes, loading and unloading kilns, etc.

WORK CYCLES

Since he began as a professional potter, John has always worked on a cyclical schedule. The length of the cycle is determined by how long it took to make enough pots for a bisque firing. This has varied over the years with the speed of production and size of kiln. In the early 1970s there were normally eight work cycles per year, with three to five weeks devoted to making pots, then a week or more for bisque firing, glazing, and glaze firing. The eight bisque loads yielded enough pots (about 300 to 400 in each) for ten or twelve glaze firings, so there was considerable carryover of bisque ware between cycles. John's schedule was tightly organized to allow him to produce 2500 to 3000 pots per year during

Slab-built tray with wire-cut
handle, 1975.

Slab-built tray with wire-cut
handle, 1974.

Openwork plate form, 1974, 15″ (38.1 cm) X 13″ (33 cm). This piece was constructed of separate slabs and ribbons of clay, pressed together into a single unit by a slab roller. Decoration is impressed, stamped, trailed, and brushed.

Slab-built canister set with thrown necks and lids.

six-to six-and-a-half day work weeks, with ten-to-twelve-hour working days beginning at 6:00 A.M. There were few breaks and few vacations. He was exuberant, completely immersed in his work, and excited by his productivity and the growth and development of his ideas, and left himself little time for anything else.

Although by some standards not a huge production, it should be remembered that many of the forms were complex and time-consuming to make and decorate, and that considerable time was spent developing new forms, experimenting with templates and molds, and devising new tools. Normally no more than three or four hours in a ten-hour workday would actually be devoted to throwing. During the last four years John has been writing a book and has also spent more time with his family, so the work cycles are somewhat longer, and there are fewer firings in a year. Current work cycles involve about five-to-six weeks of throwing and assembling pots. Glazing and decorating a kiln load of pots takes five or six days. Five work cycles per year yield enough pots for seven glaze firings. About four to six weeks scattered through the year are rest or vacation periods, while the rest of the time is devoted to writing, teaching, studio maintenance and repairs, and development of new tools, equipment, and technical skills. John still begins work at 6:00 A.M. but rarely works evenings and almost never on Sunday. Currently a typical workday involves eight to ten hours in the studio (less if he is working on the book). He is producing considerably less, but is still able to earn a comfortable living and is now taking more time to enjoy his family and pursue a variety of other interests. His more relaxed work schedule is allowing him to have a more satisfying and integrated life, but the compulsive drive both to produce quantities of pots and to work out his new ideas is still there.

SALES

From the beginning John has been committed to a direct sales approach because he receives full value return on sales, has greater creative freedom, and values the feedback from direct contact with his customers. About 85 percent of John's sales are directly to retail customers, mostly through his studio showroom. John

John:
I knew that the productivity of the studio would be less and accepted that. The studio has not dried up from lack of nourishment. My ideas are still as exciting to me. I can't realize them as fast as I used to, but they don't go away, although I do feel frustrated at times. I have had to fight against the tendency to make simple pots that are easy to deal with in order to get a kiln load finished in the same time frame I used to. I have had to suppress that sense of urgency and continue to take the time to work out the ideas, and devote the same attention to details and decoration. Being an almost compulsive decorator is at the same time terribly exciting and frustratingly confining. My enthusiasm for developing a train of thought always runs headlong into the inevitable prolonged sessions of decorating—something I simply must do, but am very much aware of in terms of time.

Glick's art fair units.

84

does no wholesaling but does supply pots on consignment to two galleries, one in Chicago and one near Detroit. For several years art fairs were important sales outlets for John, and in some years, fairs accounted for as much as 35 percent of total retail sales. Although he never attended more than five in one year, he has exhibited at most of the major Midwest fairs in Chicago, Milwaukee, and Ann Arbor, as well as smaller fairs in Michigan, which also generate additional business at his studio. Since 1975 he has gone to no more than one fair each year and does not plan to increase his involvement in the foreseeable future. The showroom is open only four days a week (Wednesday through Friday afternoons and Saturday from 10 A.M. to 5 P.M.). Sales are usually handled by Ruby. Things that are most popular, or least popular, and comments made by customers are factors taken into account in determining production. However, John's own interests and feelings are paramount.

There is just a small sign beside the road at the entrance to the pottery, and John does only occasional advertising (usually mailings to previous customers). These have ranged from simple announcements or notices to elaborate illustrated brochures. His best advertising is word of mouth, which has steadily built his clientele during his 12 years at the Plum Tree Pottery. For years many customers return over and over. Often there is disappointment when a certain series or type of work is no longer available, but there is also fascination with the continual development of new ideas, which tends to create new demand old customers.

Pricing. When he first started as a professional, John's pricing was influenced by other potters' prices, and he used these as a guide to price his own work. After about six months he began doing time studies, determining how much time was spent on each pot, forming, trimming, decorating, and glazing, in an effort to arrive at a price accurately reflecting the work that went into it. But as his work was continually changing, he gradually developed a looser, more complex, partly logical, partly intuitive pricing method that took into account approximate time spent as well as size, sales success, and comparative quality. Sometimes the price of a type of ware is arbitrarily increased to slow demand relative to other pieces in order to maintain a balance. Occasionally pieces that John feels are especially successful may be priced higher than other similar ones, or those that are technically sound but less esthetically inspired, may be lower in price than normal.

Generally his aim is to arrive at prices that seem fair and equitable to customers and provide a reasonable profit over the entire production, although individual pieces may vary in their percentage of return. For example, the types of teapots John is currently making actually require more than twice as much time as large bowls, but a reasonable asking price is no more than half as much.

John:
I listen to me first—emotionally, esthetically—then do what pleases me. Market considerations are secondary. Making only what is popular in one's work quickly becomes a habit, then a dead end. My ideas develop best in an atmosphere where I do what seems interesting and provocative for me— do it first purely for my enjoyment, then offer it in the showroom.

ANALYSIS OF WORK

John produces a large variety of pots, almost all of them functional, including teapots, casseroles and baking dishes, bowls, plates, platters, mugs, cups, lidded boxes and jars, corked jars, canister sets, pitchers, wine bottles, tureens, soap dishes, and planters. These forms are continually changing and evolving. Some shapes are traceable through numerous subtle stages of evolution over a period of years, while others may develop and disappear within a few weeks or months.

John pursues an idea through many variations for as long as it is stimulating for him. When a particular form or decorative idea no longer excites him, he moves on to another. He knows that for his work to remain at its best, he must feel an excitement in making it, and in order to remain true to himself and, ultimately, to his customers, he must continue to develop new ideas and discard those that no longer interest and stimulate him.

Changes are rarely sudden but are the result of a gradual evolutionary process, constantly building on past experience. During his student years, outside influences were often significant factors in his development, but recently his ideas have become more and more internal, each stage sowing the seeds of the next.

More than half of his output is thrown, but a substantial portion is slab-built or a combination of thrown and slab elements. John's throwing is sure, fluid, natural, and easy—casual but never careless. Large forms are thrown on chipboard bats; small ones, off the hump. Trimming is minimal; most forms are cut with a twisted cord from the bat or hump, with a refinement of the edge as the only trimming. Dinnerware sets usually have trimmed foot rings, while similar pieces, not part of a set, rarely are treated this way. John's thrown forms are almost always basically simple, although many are altered, faceted or carved, or have sculptural handles or other additions.

The slab-built pots range from quite simple oval and square forms to complex irregular and assymetrical ones. Slab forms are always done in series, many of them developed and refined to a standard size and shape. Then John makes templates and sometimes wooden press molds that allow an assistant to efficiently duplicate the basic form, which John then completes, decorates, and glazes. Recently John has developed several series based on extruded slabs of various decorative configurations. Most of the forms have been boxes with lid flanges incorporated into the extrusions. All of the slab series are produced in limited numbers for as long as they continue to stimulate him to make new variations in refining, detailing, decorating, adding spouts, handles, etc. A given work cycle might include four to six editions of eight to twelve pieces each. Usually no more than 100 to 150 examples of a given form are made over a two or three year period.

John's pots are bold, vigorous, and exuberant, enriched with lively, varied, sometimes whimsical decoration, and a lush richness of color. Their initial impact is forceful and direct, yet they are rich in subtle nuance and detail in form, surface, pattern, and color, inviting lingering contemplation.

Glazes and Decoration. John's use of decorative techniques and glaze combinations in the last few years has grown continually richer and more complex. He is currently using 30 to 32 glazes: 18 celadon type glazes (four basic formulas with color variations), several slip and ash glazes, and a few matt glazes. During a glazing and decorating period the large buckets of glaze, normally stored under shelves and tables in the throwing area, are lined up on two long parallel tables so that John can move freely up and down between them, applying the various combinations of glazes in quick succession. Glazing is done by dipping and pouring, with most pots receiving overlapping combinations of two to four glazes, some as many as five. The different glazes combined with slips applied over the raw glaze produce myriad color variations.

He makes notes on glaze results after each firing, and before

John:
There are too many fresh ideas. I have too many sheaves of sketches, too many frustrations in not having time to follow through new ideas to want to perpetuate something that has lost its excitement for me. I am keenly aware that using this approach I am bound to make some unsuccessful pots, but it's the price I will pay for the freedom I enjoy.

Wine bottle, 1973, 18″ (46 cm) high. Slab-built body, with thrown top, threaded stopper, and pulled handle.

glazing often refers to these and examines recent pots in order to refresh his memory and stimulate his thinking. However, he does not use the notes as guides or formulas to be duplicated as much as starting points for further development. Preferring to work spontaneously and intuitively, he arrives sometimes almost by chance at new achievements, rather than precluding them by safely freezing his work at a certain stage. He feels that continuously repeating combinations he knows will produce good results will eventually lead to lifeless pots.

Usually several different decorative techniques are used on each piece. The still-wet pot may be decorated by impressing or incising, followed by irregular applications of white or colored slip that is patterned by drawing with a stiff brush, broom straws, wooden tools, or by pressing a patterned sponge stamp into the wet slip and lifting off (by absorption) part of the coating. When the piece is a little stiffer, decorative sculptural additions are attached and incised details are added or refined. After bisque firing and glazing, the pot may be further decorated with oxides (iron, cobalt, rutile, copper) applied with brushes or sponge printed over layers of raw glaze. The fusion of color and pattern that appears after glaze firing has a sensuous depth and richness, the various elements blending together in subtle, elusive, contrapuntal relationships. Occasionally clarity is obscured by an excess of detail, or a profusion of color becomes somewhat muddy, but these are problems John accepts in his continual exploration and innovation.

Despite the sometimes baroque extravagance of form and detail, functional considerations are not neglected. John's massive sculptural handles are well balanced and comfortable to hold; eccentric teapot spouts pour cleanly and smoothly; lids fit precisely. Usual proportions and configurations often provide a tactile experience as surprising and delightful as their appearance. It should be noted, however, that many of John's pots are simple and conventional in form and function and derive their unique character from surface decoration.

Teapots. John's way of working can be traced in the evolution of his teapots, a form that has continued to fascinate him for many years. They are also among the most spectacular examples of his imaginative use of many elements, combining a strong sculptural form with elaborate, sometimes whimsical detailing and rich patterns and colors. The teapot at its simplest is an inevitably complex form. John has created a wide range of variations, achieving strongly sculptural forms through manipulation, exaggeration, and embellishment of spouts, handles, and lids, as well as the body itself. His early teapots were fairly conventional thrown forms: full-bodied, well-proportioned, and smoothly finished. Gradually, unusual details and variations began to appear. While working on a faceted series, John felt that thrown spouts no longer seemed appropriate and began constructing S-curved four-sided slab spouts. These led to press-molded spouts of hexagonal cross section and more recently to a series of long extruded spouts. Handles have been pulled, wire-cut, press-molded, and extruded, often with added or carved details. John's interest in blacksmithing has recently led to a series of teapots incorporating forged steel handles with wood or press-molded ceramic grips. Teapot bodies have been thrown, faceted, altered, slab-built, or press-molded. The decoration involves incising, carving, im-

A group of leather-hard teapots with thrown and altered bodies, with a variety of press-molded, extruded, and wire-cut handles and spouts.

Teapot, 1973. The same body and spout as the left one, combined with a press-molded handle and different decorative treatment produce a very different pot.

Teapot with thrown and faceted body, press-molded spout and wire-cut handle, 1974.

Teapot with slab-built body formed in a wood-press mold, wire-cut handle, press-molded spout, 1973.

Teapot with thrown and faceted body, extruded spout, is
joined to a press-molded spout
base, wire-cut handle, 1977.

pressing, and sprigging; using slips that are brushed, trailed, printed, and patterned; using glazes in many combinations; and brushing or printing patterns in oxides over the raw glaze. Handles, spouts, and lids are not treated simply as harmoniously integrated functional appendages but as sculptural and decorative elements.

Occasionally, especially in transition periods, the parts do not fit quite comfortably together. But there is always a dynamic restless energy and tension, a surprising inventive twist, and a strong sculptural quality. Behind even the most whimsical and flamboyant of these pots, there is integrity, seriousness, and conviction.

COMMISSIONS

John normally refuses all commissions except dinnerware sets and (occasionally) planters for architects. He found that he could not keep up with the many and varied special requests and still remain free to develop his own ideas. Each glaze firing usually includes a dinnerware set, but they are so much in demand that customers have usually had to wait a year or more. John now estimates that it will take six years, at his present rate of production, to fill dinnerware orders from customers on his current waiting list.

Until three or four years ago, dinnerware sets were carefully matched in size and glazing, with only minor variations in decoration. The preferences of the customer were carefully considered. He could choose from many samples in the showroom (the samples were continually changing since a decorative pattern was rarely repeated), or he might specify a particular decoration with a certain glaze. If a customer wanted a specific combination not in the sample collection, a prototype setting of three pieces was made for his approval before proceeding with the actual set. John was careful to insure that the customer knew in advance exactly what he was getting. In addition, complete records, including shapes, sizes, clay weights, glazes, and decoration, were kept for each set so that satisfactory replacements or additional pieces could be made.

John has now broken away from this meticulous system, offering a more spontaneous and varied set, though the customer must relinquish control. John shows the customer samples of the directions he is currently exploring in his decoration and glazing. Sizes and shapes may be selected from several standard ones, and the customer can specify that certain glazes or colors not be used, but except for these limitations John remains as free as in his other work. The sets do not match in the usual sense, but are related as variations on a central theme. A decorative idea may be developed in many different ways, and colors may vary considerably, but an overall coherence is maintained. The new approach is more exciting and satisfying for John and, despite occasional initial resistance, for the purchaser as well.

Storage jars 1976. Thrown and faceted with incised, slip, and oxide decoration.

Covered jars with incised, sponge-printed, and brush decoration.

STEPHEN JEPSON

Jepson Pottery
GENEVA, FLORIDA

Left
Stephen always throws in a standing position. Bats and water are on a rack beside the wheel, freshly thrown pots are set on large tables to stiffen for trimming, and completed pots are transferred to ware carts.

Right
Large covered jar with graceful, spontaneous sliptrailed decoration in white under a rich, warm, tan glaze.

Since 1971 Stephen Jepson has been a professional potter, and since 1973, has been working in his present studio near the quiet village of Geneva, Florida, about 25 miles northeast of Orlando. This part of central Florida is mostly undeveloped and rural: a broad, flat, open landscape of marshland, lakes, pastures, and forests of pines and palms, and citrus groves. Stephen and his wife Martha live about a mile from the studio in a modest but spacious house overlooking a small lake surrounded by pine trees. Isolated amid their 55 acres that embrace fields, woods, a 17-acre citrus grove, and part of the lake, they rarely hear a sound louder than the breeze through the trees.

Stephen is assisted in the studio by Martha and one part-time and three full-time employees. Together they produce a large volume of functional and decorative pottery, both thrown and slab-built, which is almost all sold either at art fairs or wholesale to shops, galleries, and department stores. Stephen and Martha normally work in the studio seven days a week, except when traveling, which is almost entirely for business. They drive their van 50,000 miles a year, mostly to art fairs and for wholesale deliveries. They enjoy traveling, but seldom take time for sightseeing along the way and rarely take a real vacation.

Financially very successful, Stephen has already far surpassed his original goal of making a modest but comfortable living, and at the age of 33 set himself the goal of becoming a millionaire within ten years. With six years left, he feels he is well underway and somewhat ahead of schedule. After age 43 he plans to take more time to relax and travel for pleasure, though one can only be skeptical since what he enjoys most of all is making pottery, and he will undoubtedly be hard at work on his next ten-year plan.

For several years he has taught evening pottery classes at nearby Florida Technical University. He is not dependent on the income, but enjoys teaching and is especially proud of several students who have pursued graduate work in ceramics.

Stephen is intensely interested in the work of other potters and has for years been building a collection of contemporary American pottery. His collection includes pieces by some of the best potters in the country, among them John Glick and Karl Christiansen, who were early and continuing inspirations to him.

Each year he organizes workshops at his own studio, inviting nationally prominent potters to give lecture-demonstrations, to expose his students and local potters to new ideas and techniques. Participants pay a small fee to help defray expenses, which are underwritten by Stephen himself.

Casserole with thrown handle and wax-resist decoration in deep cobalt blue.

Covered cheese dish with wax-resist decoration.

BACKGROUND

Stephen had been encouraged as a child to draw and paint. He had also done clay modeling, but his first brief contact with the potter's wheel came when he was a 21-year-old zoology student at Morningside College in Iowa, preparing for medical school. However, he did not become really involved with clay until three years later at the University of Iowa, when he took a beginning pottery course under Jim McKinnell, while still (with some misgivings) following a pre-medical program. Throwing came quickly and naturally to him. He became so fascinated with clay and stimulated by the excitement he felt among the graduate students, that he abandoned any idea of becoming a doctor and devoted the next year-and-a-half to studying pottery. The following summer he studied for nine weeks with Marguerite Wildenhain in California, throwing eight hours a day, five days a week. He never kept a pot, but greatly increased his skill and speed. This intense experience was followed by a two-year period of uncertainty, during which he worked as a photographer, then a jeweler. When he finally determined that he still really wanted to be a potter, he systematically set about selecting a graduate school, visiting more than a dozen before deciding on Alfred University. Because he still did not have an undergraduate degree, he first completed his B.S. in zoology at Northeast Missouri State University, where he met his wife Martha. He also studied pottery there, became involved in ceramic sculpture, and built his first kiln. At Alfred he concentrated on functional stoneware and paid his way through graduate school with pottery sales.

Both Stephen and Martha detest cold weather, especially after two years of snow in upstate New York, so Florida seemed to them a logical place to establish a studio. In March of 1971, while still a student at Alfred, Stephen exhibited at an art fair in Winter Park and met a man who offered him a studio and living space at a nominal rent on a farm near Orlando. Stephen and Martha lived and worked there for two years before buying the site of the present studio in 1973.

The four buildings comprising the 6000-sq.-ft. studio complex (a small, simple house and three prefabricated industrial-type steel buildings set well back from the road) stand somewhat incongruously before an exotic backdrop of orange trees, palms, and a magnificent old live oak draped with Spanish moss. When the Jepsons bought the property in 1973, the only building was the small house with a large one-room addition that at first served as the main work area and is still Stephen's throwing room. The rest of the house is used as a display area.

Stephen immediately erected the first two steel buildings (each with about 1000-sq.-ft of floor space), one for the kiln, the other for storage and tools. As he hired assistants and increased his production, he needed more space and in 1975 added a third and much larger steel building, about 40 by 80 ft.

In addition to the 100-cu.-ft. car kiln, the kiln building houses clay mixing equipment: a Soldner mixer and a Bluebird pug mill. Stephen plans to add a hammer mill for processing a cheap and plentiful local clay that he hopes to use as a major ingredient in his standard body, and also for grinding discarded bisque into grog. There is also room for a small metal shop that includes welding equipment. The other small steel building is now the hand-building area, where the assistants spend much of their time. Slabs are made with a Robert Brent slab roller, and a Brent extruder is used to make handles and small coils for sprigged decoration.

Although at present only Stephen and one of his assistants throw, there are four Shimpo electric wheels and one Randall kick wheel. All are fitted to accept easily interchangeable bucket heads of two sizes, which in turn accept two sizes of flanged plaster bats, making a convenient and highly efficient system for production throwing. Because of a back injury, Stephen always throws in an erect standing position. To raise the Shimpo wheels to an appropriate height, he has built two steel stands, one incorporating a backrest structure. He normally spends seven or eight hours a day throwing, and has designed his studio for efficient production, with clay supply, wedging table, bats, shelves, and a large work table conveniently arranged around his wheel. A large blackboard near the wheel is usually filled with notes, ideas, and sketches.

To facilitate moving pots between the buildings, Stephen has built 21 steel frame-ware carts, which accept 1 by 3 ft. ware boards; all buildings are connected by floor level concrete walks. An essential piece of equipment is a large Dodge van used for making wholesale deliveries and for taking pots and display units to art fairs.

Kilns. All bisque and glaze firing is done in a 100-cu.-ft. sprung arch insulating brick car kiln that Stephen built in 1973. The car unit (door and floor) rolls out on six wheels running on steel tracks, providing complete access to the stacking area from both sides. The kiln is fired with propane at four to six pounds pressure, using ten natural draft burners that Stephen also built.

Until recently Stephen had fired to cone 10 but, to conserve fuel, has begun lowering his firing temperature, which is now cone 8, and may lower it further. He has altered his glazes to mature at the lower temperature while retaining essentially the same qualities. However, he finds that his unaltered clay body is suf-

View of the studio complex showing the original house at left, and two of the three metal buildings. The kiln building is behind the hand-building studio (center).

The 100-cu.-ft. car kiln in which bisque and glaze firing is done.

Coffeepot with thrown spout,
pulled handle, stony matt
glaze.

ficiently mature at cone 8 and is actually more resistant to thermal shock.

Because of the high humidity of the Florida climate, both glaze and bisque firings are begun with an overnight soak at low heat, reaching perhaps 500°F by 8:00 A.M. From that point a cone 8 glaze firing takes about nine hours.

ASSISTANTS

Stephen presently employs three full-time studio assistants and one who does piecework at home. The studio employees are paid by the hour and work a 35-hour week. There is considerable flexibility, and each employee can vary his hours, though most work Monday through Friday from 8:30 A.M. to 4:30 P.M., with an hour off for lunch. They are allowed five paid sick days per year, paid national holidays, and depending on length of time with the pottery, one or two weeks paid vacation, and may take longer vacations without pay. They also receive a small percentage of profits above a certain amount. Marvin Miller, a former computer programmer, has worked with Stephen since 1975, while the others have only recently joined him. In the summer of 1977 Stephen's sister, Susan Kelly, and her husband Richard moved from Iowa to Florida to work for the pottery. Susan works on a commission basis as a sales representative, while Richard, who has had some pottery experience, is one of the studio assistants.

Stephen had worked alone until he injured his back shortly after moving to the new studio in 1973, and could not throw. Fearing he might never be able to return to production throwing, he

Above
Marvin, an assistant, refines the edges of a press-molded box form.

Using glazing tongs, Martha dips pots in a large bucket of glaze, while Richard cleans drops of glaze from waxed bottoms and rims.

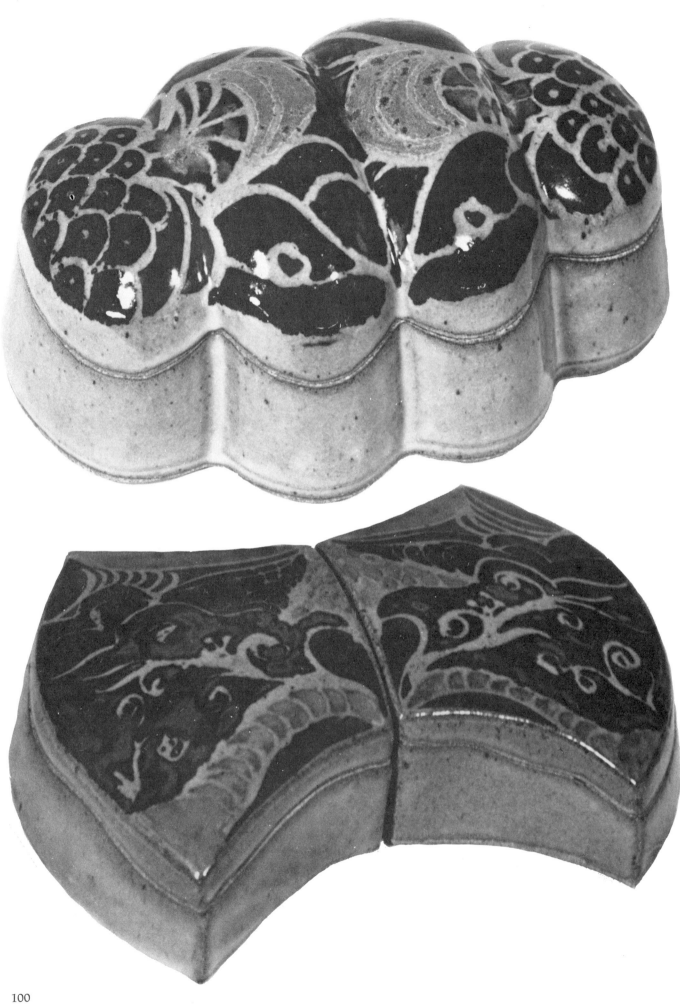

determined to use his facilities for making red clay flowerpots, hiring other people to do the throwing. He hired one of his former students, who had some throwing skill and quickly learned to make the simple standard forms. As Stephen's back improved he found he could throw standing up and returned to making stoneware. The assistant was kept on and regularly threw a number of Stephen's standard tableware pieces, as well as handbuilding, until he left in 1976. A total of eleven employees have worked in the studio since 1973, four of whom were students from a local high school cooperative education program, but never more than three at one time.

Stephen feels that the most important, appropriate, and profitable use of his time is to concentrate on the work for which only he is qualified, while delegating less skilled work as well as routine jobs to assistants. There is a very clear division of labor based on individual skills. Stephen does almost all throwing and trimming, all pulled handles, all brush decoration (although the coloring oxides are usually applied over his wax-resist patterns by Marvin or Martha), develops prototypes for all new standard pieces to be made by assistants, and always fires the kiln. The most important contribution of the assistants to actual production is the assembly of standard slab forms, including 18 different lidded boxes, formed in plaster press molds. They also do impressed and sprigged decoration following Stephen's designs. Only one, Richard, has throwing skill, and he makes the four simplest small dinnerware pieces.

Stephen spends most of the day working alone in his own studio, but often checks on the work of the assistants. He sees every piece that is made and destroys those few that he finds unacceptable technically or esthetically. He regularly discusses and criticizes in detail his employees' work with them, stressing positive qualities while pointing out specifically how the work could be improved.

Much of the day-to-day operation of the studio is supervised and organized by Martha, who, among other things, keeps track of orders and inventory, handles most of the correspondence (although Susan as sales representative is beginning to take over some of it), helps with quality control of the employees' work, schedules firings, and loads the kiln. She also does most of the glazing and makes many of the small cylindrical slab-built salt and pepper shakers that are a standard item. Assistants help with loading and unloading the kiln and handle most studio cleaning and clay and glaze preparation. They also apply oxide stains to unglazed pots, wax the bottoms of pots prior to glazing, and do some glazing. Neither Martha nor any of the present employees has any desire to be independent potters in their own right and seem happy in their roles as part of a production team.

Although pleased with the present relationships and cautious about bringing a second creative force into the studio, Stephen envisions hiring another potter, whose work he respects and who would be compatible stylistically and temperamentally, to work as a designer.

WORK CYCLES

There are no definite work cycles. Potterymaking continues during glazing and firing sequences, and the spacing of these sequences is variable and does not always closely follow production

Press-molded box with blue, red, orange, and green wax-resist decoration.

Press-molded, two-section box with wax-resist decoration in blue, red, orange, and green.

Top
Press-molded box with wax-resist decoration.

Above
Unglazed press-molded box with applied coil decoration, accented with a mixture of iron oxide and manganese dioxide.

Left
Large thrown jar with wax-resist decoration in deep cobalt blue.

Right
Dinnerware pieces including plate, saucer, and two types of soup bowl.

volume. Bisque and glaze firings are done in the same kiln, and a cycle of bisque firing, glazing, decorating, and glaze firing takes about a week. Since the time of Stephen's back injury Martha has usually handled the stacking of the kiln (sometimes assisted by one of the employees). To minimize the lifting of heavy kiln shelves, each bisque is stacked exactly as the following glaze firing will be; the shelf structure is left in place while the pots are removed, glazed, and replaced on the same shelves. Martha sometimes makes a quick diagram of the bisque load as a guide to repacking, which begins as soon as the first pots are glazed. By the time glazing and decorating are completed, the kiln is nearly loaded. Although many more pots could be fitted into the kiln for bisque firing by nesting and stacking, so that three bisque firings might yield enough pots for four glaze firings, the Jepsons have found their system efficient in terms of time and effort for them.

A maximum of four cycles per month is possible, and currently two or three firing cycles per month are required to keep abreast of normal production, which can fill the kiln in one and a half to two weeks. For various reasons a regular firing schedule is not always maintained, and five or six weekly firings may sometimes be required to catch up with production. A large backlog always results in June, when Stephen and Martha are gone most of the month to art fairs, while their employees continue working normal hours. Stephen hopes that as his assistants become more experienced, they might load and fire a bisque kiln during his absence, but does not want to relinquish personal involvement in glaze firings.

The Jepsons normally work at the studio about eight hours a day, seven days a week, and in addition Stephen teaches a two-and-a-half-hour class four evenings a week. On Saturday and Sunday, Stephen and Martha work the same schedule as on weekdays, but there is a different atmosphere since the employees are not there. Occasionally they take some time off for recreation such as sailing on a large lake near the studio.

Though not physically active work, potting does require a certain stamina and endurance. Stephen is convinced of the importance of keeping physically fit to maintain a healthy and positive mental outlook as well. To avoid the backstrain of sitting and bending over, he always stands while working, whether throwing, trimming, or decorating. He exercises for 10 to 15 minutes to warm up before starting work in the morning and after lunch, and keeps in shape with weight lifting, jumping rope, swimming, and running, often several miles a day.

SALES

In 1977 Stephen's sales were about 20 percent retail at art fairs and 80 percent wholesale to shops, galleries, and department stores. This represents a complete reversal of his sales pattern of a few years ago, when art fairs accounted for as much as 85 percent of the total sales.

Stephen began selling at local art fairs while an undergraduate and during his years at Alfred University was accepted at some of

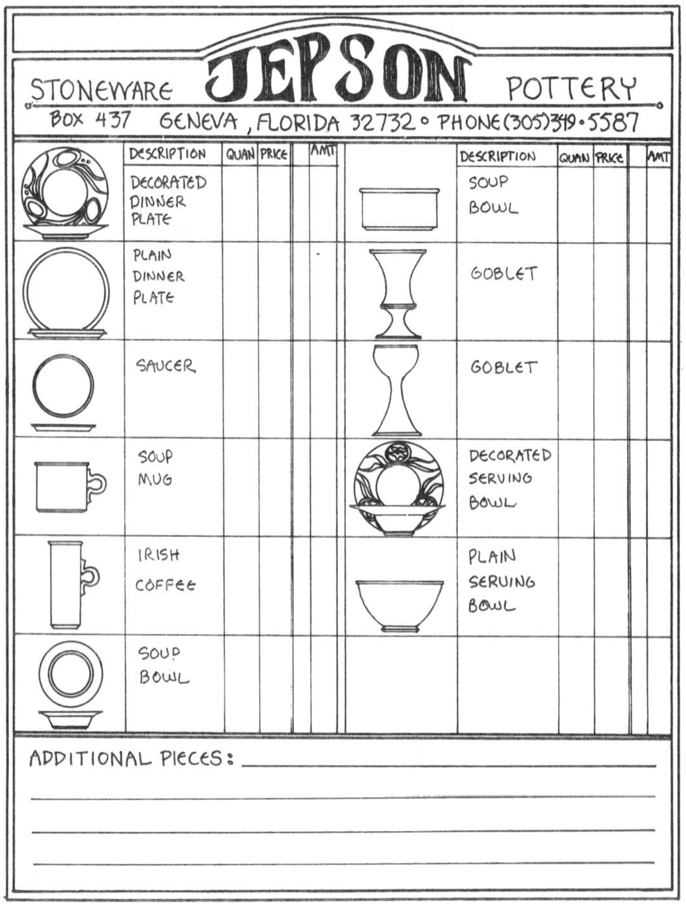

An order form from The Jepson Pottery.

STONEWARE JEPSON POTTERY
BOX 437 GENEVA, FLORIDA 32732 ○ PHONE (305) 349•5587

	DESCRIPTION	QUAN	PRICE	AMT		DESCRIPTION	QUAN	PRICE	AMT
	DECORATED DINNER PLATE					SOUP BOWL			
	PLAIN DINNER PLATE					GOBLET			
	SAUCER					GOBLET			
	SOUP MUG					DECORATED SERVING BOWL			
	IRISH COFFEE					PLAIN SERVING BOWL			
	SOUP BOWL								

ADDITIONAL PIECES: _____

_____

_____

_____

104

Small faceted bowl.

A press-molded box with decoration of applied coils, in a warm yellow matt glaze.

the larger juried fairs. He had also begun wholesaling some of his work while a student at Alfred, but established the Florida studio in 1971 with the intention of relying essentially on retail sales at art fairs. For several years his financial success was based almost exclusively on art fairs, and Stephen and Martha attended as many as 26 in one year. These included the lucrative major fairs in Chicago, Milwaukee, and Ann Arbor, in the summer, and many smaller fairs in Florida during the winter. It was not uncommon during this period for Martha to attend one fair while Stephen was at another or back at the studio firing the kiln in preparation for the next one.

Selling at fairs meant receiving the full retail price for each pot, but the cost in time and effort was immense, with as much as two months of the year spent at, or traveling to and from, fairs. After the first two years Stephen and Martha began eliminating the least profitable fairs, reducing the number they attended to 18 in 1974. Until three years ago Stephen had experienced substantial yearly increases in sales at those fairs he regularly attended, but since then, with few exceptions, sales have declined. Other potters have had this experience as well, and while possibly associated with general economic conditions, it is probably largely due to increased competition (more art fairs and more potters by their ubiquity dispersing demand more rapidly than it increases). The decrease in sales, coupled with the disadvantages of capricious weather, large crowds, and the time-consuming process itself, led Stephen to concentrate on increasing his wholesale business, while continuing to exhibit only at the fairs most profitable for him. Although each year they are tempted by one or two new fairs, they went to only ten in 1977, and this year's schedule will

Canister set, mottled blue-brown glaze.

include eight or nine. Eventually, if wholesale markets continue to expand, they may withdraw from art fairs almost completely, though they will probably continue to go to Ann Arbor because it is so profitable and Winter Park because it is a pleasant experience, reasonably profitable, and only 30 miles from their home.

Except with a cooperative gallery in Winter Park, of which he is a member, Stephen has never become involved in consignment (sale or return) arrangements, in which the potter usually receives two-thirds or more of the retail price as opposed to only one-half in conventional wholesaling. He feels that wholesaling is more professional and businesslike and eliminates the confusion and extra bookkeeping of consignment.

For several years Stephen's wholesale business has been steadily growing (partly through art fair contacts with shop and gallery buyers), but the bulk of it has been with a dozen outlets that send regular repeat orders. One of these, The Storehouse (a large furniture and handicraft store in Atlanta with eleven branches in the South), accounts for almost one-half, while his second largest outlet, to which he has been selling since he was a student at Alfred, is the American Hand (a small gallery/shop in Washington, D.C. that sells exclusively handmade pottery and glass). Many other orders come at irregular intervals, and some have been one-time sales.

As part of his effort to generate new wholesale business, Stephen's sister Susan recently began traveling with a large group of samples to galleries, shops, and department stores on the East Coast and across the South. She opened 15 new accounts on her first two trips, including a large Florida department store chain, which sent an initial $6000 order. Susan is paid a 15 percent com-

mission on her sales and on subsequent orders from accounts she has opened. She is also taking over some of the deliveries that Stephen and Martha used to make, and will help out at art fairs. Stephen has established a five percent surcharge for delivery and a $400 minimum order.

Three printed sheets with diagrammatic sketches illustrate the 11 dinnerware pieces, 28 varieties of lidded boxes, and some other standard repeat items that can be ordered. Other thrown pieces such as mugs, steins, pitchers, and cookie jars can also be ordered but may vary in form. As wholesale orders vary greatly, Stephen has not felt restricted in what he makes, even though a large percentage of his work is now ordered before it is made. Some buyers concentrate on small functional thrown pots, while others are only interested in the more elaborate and expensive decorated pieces, and still others want the greatest variety possible.

Although Stephen maintains a studio showroom, sales there account for only about two percent of the total. He has never been interested in developing it as an important retail outlet since he feels it would disrupt the daily routine of potterymaking. He has twice held a special Christmas exhibition and sale at the studio in late November, but does not plan another soon since they were only moderately successful. In addition, he is now especially busy with wholesale orders at that time of year.

Prices are standardized for all the standard production pieces, and more variable pieces are priced comparably. Wholesale prices are one-half retail prices, and about half the pots are made wholesale for $10 or less. Seconds are either destroyed or marked down and sold at the studio. Especially successful pieces are not priced differently from others, but some of these are saved for exhibitions. Stephen also keeps some representative pieces that he especially likes for his own collection, and many of these are used daily in his home.

Small press-molded cork jar.

Pottery as a Business. Stephen has a more business-oriented approach than most potters, and he tends to think and talk in business terms. He sees potterymaking not only as an exciting and satisfying way of making a living, but as a business opportunity that if properly exploited can be highly profitable. Before coming to Florida, Stephen did not envision the kind of studio, numbers of employees, and volume of production he has today, but now sees this as only a preliminary stage in the development of a much grander scale operation, the outlines of which remain vague.

Although Stephen's gradual shift from retail to wholesale markets has meant having to make many more pots just to maintain the same income, increased efficiency in production has more than offset this, and gross sales have been growing 20 to 30 percent each year. He now confidently hopes to triple his present sales in two or three years. He feels that he should be nearly able to double his production with his present facilities and perhaps one additional employee, but to go beyond that he will require a second kiln and more assistants. Stephen has carefully established a line of credit with a local bank that will enable him to get substantial unsecured loans for future expansion or to meet unforeseen difficulties.

Stephen feels his service to wholesale customers is important, and he tries to present a businesslike image and maintain a repu-

Stephen:
I used to have a limited idea of the possibilities in pottery, but my attitude has changed. Now I feel the sky is the limit. The market is there, and we're just beginning to scratch the surface.

tation for dependability, which he feels can be almost as significant in successful wholesaling as making good, saleable pottery.

He is beginning to explore areas usually scorned by potters such as national advertising, packaging, and public relations. A recent mail-order advertisement in a national magazine brought little response, but undiscouraged, he feels he has learned something from an expensive failure, and future advertising will be more carefully conceived and directed. He has commissioned packaged designs for two of his most popular standard pieces, with the idea of making them attractive in markets not normally associated with handmade pottery. The designs are still tentative, but he is already considering the possibilities of special packaging for other pieces as well. He has consulted a public relations expert on ways to increase his sales, but as yet no specific plans have developed from this. He reads a great deal about sales and business methods, and is full of ideas for investments of capital earned from pottery sales.

ANALYSIS OF WORK

Stephen himself makes a prodigious amount of pottery, but a large percentage of the standard production is partially or entirely made by assistants. He feels, however, that since the designs are all his and he maintains close control of the production of his employees, it is justifiable to consider each piece as his own.

There is no distinction made in marking or pricing based on whether or not Stephen has entirely or partially made a piece. All are stamped Jepson (none are signed) and priced according to a standard scale. For purposes of analysis, however, the production can be divided into the following three categories.

1. Pieces made entirely by Stephen. These include almost all of the thrown pots. Glazing is done by Martha or assistants, but decoration is done by Stephen.

2. Pieces made by assistants and decorated by Stephen. These are slab-built (press-molded) pieces, mostly lidded box forms, decorated with wax-resist or direct brushwork.

3. Pieces made entirely by assistants. These include slab pieces (most of them made in press molds) either undecorated or with impressed or sprigged decoration, and some simple undecorated thrown pots.

Types of Pots. All of the thrown pots except four standard forms (cups, soup mugs, and two bowl shapes) are made by Stephen. These include standard dinnerware (plates, bowls, and goblets) and less standardized, but consistent pieces such as pitchers of graduated sizes, mugs, steins, bowls, lidded jars of various sizes and shapes, casseroles, covered cheese dishes, and canister sets, all made regularly in large series. Teapots, coffee pots, and lamp bases as well as a variety of other forms are thrown less regularly in small groups. Stephen is excited and happy in his work, and although he is most enthusiastic about large decorated pieces, he also takes great pleasure in making a hundred mugs or small pitchers. Though quickly and efficiently thrown, each piece is carefully considered and beautifully made.

The assistants regularly make 18 different lidded box forms in press molds. The top and sides are formed in the mold, a flat bottom is added, and the resulting closed form is cut in two to form lids and base. The cut is undulating and slanted so the lid is held in place without a flange. There are various sizes and shapes including oval, hexagonal, octagonal, and lobed forms. Some of the largest and most elaborate are actually two or three boxes that fit together to make a single form. Some of the boxes are made in two or three versions (some undecorated, some with sprigged coil decoration, and others with wax resist) making a total of 28 standard pieces. In addition, there are several other large complex box forms that are occasionally made in limited numbers. Other press-molded pieces include small cork jars, square trays, oval platters, and large lobed jars for which Stephen throws lids. Salt and pepper shakers and covered jars with impressed decoration are slab-built without molds. All of the hand-built pieces were designed by Stephen, who made the prototypes and the models from which plaster molds were cast. Because of their complexity, some of the box forms could only be realized through the process of making a solid model, then casting a mold from it. Others could be made without molds, but most would require too much time to be practical production pieces.

With few exceptions the pots are skillfully crafted and carefully finished. The thrown forms generally tend to be simple, even severe, but the throwing technique is fluid and relaxed. Most pieces are designed and thrown so as to require only minimal trimming. Handles are graceful and comfortable to hold, spouts pour well, and lids fit precisely. The press-molded boxes are well made and carefully finished, but some of the other slab pieces betray, in details, a lack of real potter's skill on the part of the assistants.

Unusual care is taken to insure smooth surfaces that will be pleasant to handle and will not scratch furniture. Bone-dry pots are lightly rubbed with an abrasive-surfaced pad to remove roughness and burrs without destroying the natural surface. After the glaze firing, unglazed bottoms as well as seats and edges of lids are smoothed with valve-grinding compound.

Glazes and Decoration. Six standard glazes are normally in use at a given time, while others are used occasionally. Because Stephen has lowered his firing temperature, some switching has occurred, and he has been able to alter some glazes to mature at the lower temperature better than others. The present standard glazes include a dry stony matt, a rich mottled yellow, a buttery satin tan, and a dark rich brown-black, all used for undecorated ware, and a white semi-matt for brush-decorated ware. All produce smooth, well-developed, and generally flawless results.

Except for three small boxes whose relief decoration comes from the press molds themselves, decoration is not standardized. Two types of decoration are done by assistants: impressed patterns made with pieces of burlap lace and crocheted work, and sprigged designs made with small extruded coils attached with slip and light paddling. Assistants follow designs made by Stephen but, after some experience, are allowed limited freedom to develop variations of their own.

Brush decoration, both wax-resist and direct, is all done by Stephen. On dinnerware he follows with only minor variations a few basic patterns, but on other pieces he develops a greater variety of themes and compositions. He tends to treat each form somewhat differently, although a few ubiquitous motifs appear in many compositions. The richest and most complex brush decoration is

Stephen decorating with wax resist.

Small press-molded boxes with wax-resist decoration.

Press-molded box with wax-resist decoration, 6" (15.2 cm) long.

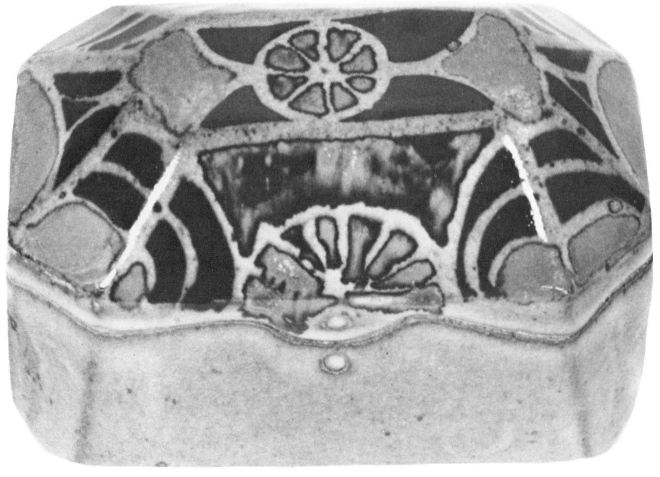

111

Stephen:
We don't produce the same thing day after day, year after year, although there are some items that we have been making for a long time. But the designs have changed gradually. We develop new things naturally as ideas evolve, but I don't feel pressured to continually come up with something new. Each year I make thousands of pots and feel that I grow infinitesimally with each one and that each year my pottery becomes stronger, more refined, and more varied.

Wax-resist decorated plates.

Small pitchers of three standard sizes.

seen on the larger box forms, on which he sometimes juxtaposes several distinct patterns in contrasting colors. Still, some of the best are also the simplest: a few quick sweeping strokes, one color with a banded accent of another. He works quickly without guidelines or sketches, although at his work table he keeps some pots with especially successful decoration as references or reminders of ideas he wants to repeat or develop further. He begins painting with a basic idea in mind, but allows details to develop spontaneously in execution.

Stephen uses only one glaze for brush-decorated pieces—an opaque white semi-matt, which develops especially rich and intense colors with the coloring oxides applied over it. He uses four colorant mixtures: a rich iron red, a deep cobalt blue, a bright crystalline orange from a mixture of iron and rutile, and a strong chrome green. The iron oxide is simply mixed with water, while small amounts of glaze and fluxes are added to the others to achieve the desired color development and insure a smooth surface. On thrown pieces he most often uses just one or two colors, but on the slab boxes (even some of the smallest ones) he normally combines three or four. He has softened the chrome green (which many potters avoid because of its hard, heavy, dominating quality), and by using it sparingly in combination with intense blue, bright red, and orange he achieves rich and dramatic results.

Stephen occasionally does slip trailed decoration, usually working with white slip on damp pots in a somewhat looser, less formal style than his brushwork. This technique, however, has not become a part of his regular production.

Stephen's work is strongly influenced by other pottery—both contemporary and historical—and he openly proclaims his eclecticism and does not hesitate to credit his sources. The influences are sometimes obvious, sometimes subtle, but always incorporated into his own style with results often surprisingly different from his sources.

The market is also an important influence on Stephen's work, but he tries to be responsive without becoming subservient. He retains his independence to develop new ideas that intrigue him, irrespective of their sales potential, but is not interested in making a lot of pots he can't sell.

Because of the nature and scale of the operation, many pieces are repeated with little change in form and decoration over a long period. There is, however, a gradual evolution in the thrown work and in the decoration, and new slab pieces are regularly developed and old ones discontinued. There is, despite standardization of many forms, a continually increasing variety as well as increasing volume.

Stephen:
The market has always spoken to me. Some of my pieces are conceived as saleable items produced quickly, simply, and sold inexpensively, but I also develop designs for many new pieces which are not predicated on how well I think they will sell. I make them first because I am interested in realizing those designs in clay, but I don't make many until I have tested the market response by offering them for sale at art fairs or to wholesale buyers.

WILHELM AND ELLY KUCH

Töpferei Kuch
BURGTHANN, WEST GERMANY

Left
Willy decorates spontaneously, rapidly combining broad, bold strokes and lively, sometimes intricate details.

Right
Large square tray with wax-resist decoration with white slip under mottled blue-brown glaze, 12½" (32 cm) across.

Wilhelm and Elly Kuch operate a large and efficient studio in Burgthann, a village 15 miles south of Nürnberg, West Germany. The pottery has grown from a primitive beginning in 1948 in a garage next to Willy's father's house into a spacious well-equipped studio. The Kuchs employ ten apprentices and assistants, and their production includes a varied line of standard ware, as well as their own individual work. Almost the entire production is sold retail from the studio showrooms or from their shop in Nürnberg.

Since the age of eight, Willy has lived in their present house (now remodeled and enlarged), which is adjacent to the studio. Their children, Mathias (now a potter with his own studio) and Katrin (studying metalsmithing) have also grown up there. A spacious and severely simple house architecturally, it is enriched with paintings, prints, weavings, furniture, and pottery reflecting the Kuchs' eclectic and discerning tastes.

Although they work long hours, Elly and Willy live comfortably, even luxuriously, and travel extensively. They have traveled all over Europe but are especially fascinated by Mediterranean culture (and sunshine) and usually prefer to vacation in Southern Europe. They have also visited Mexico and North Africa, and Elly has traveled in the United States, where she also attended a ceramics symposium. They exhibit in and attend numerous exhibitions of contemporary pottery and travel every year to the international exhibition in Faenza, Italy, where they have won six awards (first prize twice).

Their work is influenced by many things: natural objects, landscapes, travel, the work of painters (notably Klee and Bissier) and

Elly attaches a thrown
top to a slab bottle.

other potters (both historical and contemporary). They freely and openly use or adapt whatever is meaningful to them, knowing that it will be transformed as it is incorporated into their own work.

Elly and Willy intensely enjoy their work and share a deep commitment to excellence and to continuing development of new ideas and techniques. For Willy, success as a potter involves balancing three factors.

Willy:
First, in making pottery one must consider the material side. We have to be able to sell what we make, because that means freedom. Second is the enjoyment of the making process, and finally there must be a feeling of fulfillment, of satisfying the artistic spirit, a pride in the work.

BACKGROUND

Twenty years old at the end of World War II, Willy had aspired to be a painter. However, through the influence of a well-known German potter, Georg Reuss, he developed an interest in ceramics that soon became an obsession. Willy studied with Reuss in his studio for two months, but acquired little practical training, since raw materials and fuel for a kiln were difficult or impossible to obtain because of postwar shortages. He did, however, develop an appreciation for Oriental pottery, beautiful glazes, and a feeling for form, as well as an uncompromising belief in high standards—both technical and esthetic.

Willy's impatience to fire some of his work soon drove him to build a small wood-fired kiln behind his father's house in Burgthann. He still has one of the small simple pots fired in this kiln with a glaze utilizing lead and iron from an old automobile battery. Within a short time Willy had converted his father's garage into a studio, built a wheel from salvaged materials, and acquired a small electric kiln through trading combs (made in a small factory owned by his mother and uncle) for iron certificates, and these in turn traded for the kiln. Many of the first pots were

Small standard bowl with brush decoration in iron red on brown glaze, 7½″ (14 cm) in diameter.

Small standard jar with brush decoration by Willy, 5½″ (14 cm) high.

Left and below
Bottles and vase combining
slab and thrown parts. Made
and decorated with impressed
patterns by Elly, the tallest 8½''
(22 cm) high.

Right
Bottles thrown by Elly, brush-
decorated by Willy, the tallest is
8½'' (22 cm) high.

Bottom right
Covered jar with olive green
glaze, decoration in black and
white slip, 6½'' (16.5 cm) high.

bartered locally for food or other necessities rather than sold. But after the monetary reform in 1948, the beginning of economic recovery, wide-scale rebuilding, and a new prosperity in Germany, Willy soon found a ready market for all the pottery he could produce.

For the first two years Willy worked alone, gradually developing his skill and knowledge through experience, with the aid of the few technical books available at that time. In 1950 Willy was joined for a short time by his brother, who had studied pottery at a school in Nürnberg, and the studio was expanded to include a second garage and a henhouse. Elly grew up in Nürnberg and had studied pottery and later goldsmithing before marrying Willy and becoming his partner in 1951.

STUDIO AND EQUIPMENT

The Kuchs' spacious studio adjacent to their house on a hillside was built in two stages on the site of Willy's original garage studio. In 1956 the three small buildings then comprising the studio were replaced with a new two-story masonry structure. The new building's basement opened onto the downhill street level and its main floor windows looked out over village rooftops to the river valley and forested hills beyond. In 1967 an addition was built to house a studio for Elly and to provide a large open floor space for Willy to work on sculptural pieces, especially murals. This second-floor studio has windows overlooking a hillside garden and

Top right
A corner of the students' throwing and decorating room.

Bottom right
A corner of the showroom.

The street in front of the studio.

From Kuch's terraced hillside garden, the view extends over the rooftops to the river valley and the forested hills beyond. The tile roof in the foreground is Kuch's house, the flat roof is part of the studio.

opens, at the uphill end, onto a secluded terrace that can become extra work space in good weather. There are two wheels: a motorized kick wheel and a Shimpo electric.

The studio spaces are logically divided according to function, with clay mixing and storage in the basement; throwing, glazing, decorating, kiln room, and display rooms on the main floor; and Elly's studio, another showroom, and storage space on the second floor. Clay and slip preparation is done in the basement, where raw materials and processed clay are stored. There are three revolving drum-type mixers, three pug mills, a paint mixer for slip, and large concrete bins for slaking down scrap clay.

The main entrance to the studio opens into the display area from a raised terrace, where large planters are displayed. There are two gallery-like showrooms with built-in compartmented shelving, all white and dramatically illuminated, with most pots arranged in small groups similar in form, decoration, technique, or materials. The first showroom displays mostly individual pieces by Elly and Willy. The second, recently remodeled from a stock room with new shelving, paneling, and lighting, displays mostly the standard production ware, although there is some intermixing. Upstairs, a former storeroom is now a stock room with standard ware crowded and stacked upon shelves.

In addition to the showrooms, the main floor houses the principal production facilities: the throwing room, glazing and decorating room, and kiln room. The bright but somewhat crowded front room, where most of the students and employees spend much of their time, has eight motorized kick wheels and a long work bench arranged under windows along three walls. The center of the room is occupied by a massive bank of shelves holding ware awaiting trimming or decorating.

The glazing and decorating room contains a spray booth, large buckets of standard glazes for dipping and pouring, shelves lined with small batches of experimental glazes, and banks of shelves full of pots awaiting decorating, glazing, or firing. There is also a live but usually motionless iguana in a lighted glass cage.

Kilns. Ware carts can be pushed directly from this glazing room into the kiln room, where six kilns are ranked along two walls. There are five electric kilns: one 70-cu.-ft., three 35-cu.-ft. (one of which is being rebuilt as a gas kiln), and a 44-cu.-ft. car kiln. A 35-cu.-ft. gas kiln was installed in 1971 to make reduction firing possible. Up to that time all ware was oxidation-fired in the electric kilns, although occasionally for a special effect on sculptural pieces, glaze reduction or fuming was achieved by introducing naphthalene into the chamber during cooling. When the gas kiln was first installed, there was a transition period in which much of the standard ware continued to be fired in the electric kilns. But now almost all glaze firing (except for one standard dinnerware pattern and commissions utilizing bright oxidation colors) is done in the gas kiln. The electric kilns are used mostly for bisque firing and for unglazed garden ceramics.

The gas kiln, built by Riedhammer, a Nürnberg manufacturer of industrial kilns, is sophisticated, rugged, and reliable. The six burners (three at two opposite corners) are equipped with electrically ignited pilots and safety shutoff valves and are connected to a single blower. Instrumentation measures flue draft as well as gas and air pressure. Reduction can be precisely controlled, and a specified rate of temperature advance can be pre-set. Firings are

The gas kiln is loaded with glazed ware and fired three times a week.

Standard ware pitchers with trailed decoration in cobalt blue under white glaze, the tallest is 7½″ (19 cm) high.

Standard ware teapot and cups with trailed decoration in cobalt blue under white glaze, teapot 6″ (15.2 cm) high excluding handle.

Hely, an assistant, decorates a large bisque plate with glaze trailed from a rubber bulb.

Below
Standard ware platter with trailed decoration in iron red under white glaze, 16½" (43 cm) in diameter.

predictable and consistent and require little attention. Through experimentation and experience Willy has developed a ten-hour firing cycle that along with rapid cooling makes three glaze firings per week possible. He begins reduction at cone 015, continuing to the end of firing. When the kiln has reached a peak temperature (Seger cone 10–11) the gas is turned off, but the blower remains on, forcing air through the kiln, which can be opened 12 hours after the end of the firing. Although many potters feel that a long cycle is necessary for optimum results, the Kuchs' glazes are smooth and well developed, the colors rich and vibrant, and there is no cracking attributable to the rapid heating and cooling.

ASSISTANTS

The Kuchs have taken students or apprentices since 1953. They normally stay for three years, preparing for their *Gesellenprüfung* (a government-administered written and practical examination that qualifies them as journeymen potters). After three years of experience, they are eligible to take a master's examination (*Meisterprüfung*), which qualifies them to train students in their own workshops. For several years the Kuchs have normally had five or six students, which means that no more than two are accepted each year. Until recent years there were not many applications, but now there may be 100 for each opening, from Germany as well as other countries. Applicants are judged on the basis of previous artwork, enthusiasm, and personality. The Kuchs like to have one foreign student in the studio, since they feel the contact is broadening for their students as well as for themselves.

Most of the students begin at the age of 21, although some are younger. A student is normally taken for a three-month trial period, at the end of which, assuming the arrangement has proved mutually satisfactory, a three-year contract is signed. The student may leave before the expiration of the contract, but the master is obliged to keep him for three years. Most students have had art experience but usually do not have pottery skills when they come. Usually after one or two weeks, however, they are able to do some simple throwing and begin to be a part of the production team. The students are paid about $20 to $25 per week. Technical skills, shop routine, glaze and clay preparation, kiln stacking, etc., are largely learned from older students or employees. Elly and Willy are very much aware of the students' progress and criticize their work and discuss quality and design with them.

Students are expected to spend 40 hours per week in the workshop, but may set their own hours within reason. Most, however, work normal hours (8 A.M.–4 P.M. or 9 A.M.–5 P.M. Monday to Friday). They may also work on their own pots in their spare time, using studio facilities and materials. These pots are their own property, and they are free to sell them if they wish, but they are encouraged to use this as an opportunity for personal growth and development and not simply a means of earning money by turning out repeat ware.

There are now five employees, mostly former students. One of them has been with the Kuchs for 15 years, and another for 12. This year another student will be kept on as an employee. As the Kuchs want to keep the total number of people to ten, one less student will be taken this year. They could easily have phased out students, gradually replacing them with people who wanted to stay on, which would result in a more stable, efficient production

Top
Plate with wax-resist decoration, iron red glaze over white, 16″ (41 cm) in diameter.

Above
Slab-built bottle with wire-cut neck, ash glaze, 9″ (23 cm) high.

team, but they enjoy the freshness, excitement and new ideas that the younger students bring.

WORK CYCLES

There are no work cycles since the ample space in the studio, the scale of production, and number of people involved make it possible to continue all phases of potterymaking simultaneously. Most days there are people engaged in throwing, trimming, glazing, decorating, and loading or unloading kilns. At present, the gas kiln is fired with glazed ware every Monday, Wednesday, and Friday, and is unloaded and restacked every Tuesday, Thursday, and Saturday or Sunday. The addition of a second gas kiln, now under construction, will allow greater flexibility in the firing schedule. Loading and unloading of kilns is done by assistants, but Willy specifies what is to go into each firing and is intermittently present during unloading to check on results. Every week there are also several bisque firings in the electric kilns. The production is organized by Willy, who assigns work to each person, but except for new students who need more personal attention and supervision, the operation almost seems to run itself, with everyone busy and productive. The atmosphere remains relaxed and congenial.

The Kuch's shop in Nürnberg is just inside the medieval city wall, part of which can be seen above the roof.

Willy, bursting with dynamic energy, yet precise and methodical, accomplishes a prodigious amount of work, beginning at 7:30 or 8:00 A.M. and sometimes continuing after dinner in the evening. Saturday is often a normal working day, while Sunday usually involves several hours in the studio. Most of the pottery, both individual pieces and standard production ware, is glazed by spraying. Willy does all of this himself as well as decorating most of the pots made by Elly and some of the production ware. In the late 1960s when he was doing many architectural commissions, Willy gave up throwing in favor of decorating, glazing, and designing and making the large commissions. Although he is now less interested in commissions, he has not gone back to throwing, preferring to concentrate on decorating and glazing.

Elly, following much the same schedule as Willy, makes all of the individual pots and small sculptures, usually working alone in her upstairs studio, although one or two students often work there. Normally she is not involved with the standard production ware, except in rush periods such as early December. A live-in maid and cook does most of the housecleaning, shopping, and cooking except on weekends.

SALES

For several years the entire production of the workshop has been sold (except for pieces sold at exhibitions) at the studio showroom or at a small shop in Nürnberg that the Kuchs opened in 1971. In the early years a large percentage of the work was sold through a gallery in Cologne. But in the late 1950s, as the Kuchs became better known (and more Germans had automobiles), an ever-increasing amount was sold at the studio in Burgthann. The Kuchs do not advertise and there is no sign, but over the years they have built a faithful clientele.

The shop in Nürnberg was opened in 1971 as part of the *Handwerkerhof*, a complex of shops built by the city of Nürnberg in the historic Waffenhof, just inside the medieval city wall. The small half-timber, tile-roofed shops include a bakery, toy shop, and restaurant as well as other crafts shops. This shop reaches customers who would not come to Burgthann, such as tourists, and acquaints additional people with their work, who later become regular customers. A full range of current production is kept in stock at this shop, although there are comparatively fewer large pieces and sculptures and more small inexpensive pieces than at Burgthann. One section of the shop is set up as a studio with a wheel and even a small electric kiln for bisque firing. The shop is usually tended on a rotating basis by one of the students or Willy's sister-in-law. They demonstrate throwing, handle sales, and maintain the inventory of pots by taking along a few from Burgthann on each trip into Nürnberg.

Pricing. Prices are determined partially on the basis of time and effort, materials, firing, and partially on relative quality. The standard ware produced by the students and employees has standard prices that vary little except for particularly successful pieces, which will be priced higher, and esthetically or technically marred pieces, which are sold as seconds at reduced prices. The prices of Elly and Willy's individual work are considerably higher and tend to vary much more. Because there is greater variety in form and decoration, the work is continually changing. Also, a considerable disparity in time and effort is involved in various

Elly:
The contact with our customers is important for us. Many come regularly several times a year, and we couldn't adjust to selling anonymously through galleries or shops again.

Goblets with decoration in iron red on white glaze. The first two (left) were brush-decorated by Willy; the other two (right) were standard patterns done by assistants.

types of pots, so the prices are determined more subjectively. The Kuchs' feeling about the relative success of each pot is an important factor, often colored by excitement over a new idea or glaze, and an exceptional piece may cost twice as much as others of the same series. Prices of ware sent to the Nürnberg shop are slightly higher to compensate for greater overhead. Pieces sent to exhibitions are normally priced higher, but this reflects the belief that they are exceptionally successful.

ANALYSIS OF WORK

There are three distinctly different types of work produced by the Kuch studio: the standard repeat ware made and mostly decorated by the apprentices and employees; the individual pieces (mostly functional or decorative pots and some small sculptures) made by Elly, which are glazed and often decorated by Willy; and the commissioned murals and large sculptures for private homes and public buildings made by Willy. Pots are not signed; repeat ware is marked with a studio stamp, while the individual work is simply stamped "Kuch."

For years the Kuchs produced oxidation-fired stoneware and developed very rich and beautiful oxidation glazes. When the gas kiln was installed in 1971, they made a quick transition to reduction firing, though much of the standard ware continued to be oxidation-fired for several years. Although few glazes are regularly used and most standard ware is glazed with one of three glazes (a fourth is used only for dinnerware), the Kuchs are continuously experimenting with new glazes and colorants. Some of these glazes may be used only on a particular series or group of pots, while others may find their way into regular use.

Production Ware. The standard production ware designed by Elly and Willy combines simple, quiet, straightforward forms with decoration that is often elaborate and complex. Most are thrown from weighed balls of clay, using a height or width gauge to ensure uniformity. Small vertical forms such as cups, mugs, pitchers, and jars are cut off the wheel head and are not trimmed. Bowls, plates, and platters are thrown on bats and have trimmed foot rings. There are also goblets made from separately thrown stem and bowl, casseroles, and medium-to-very-large pitchers and planters. In addition to the functional pots there are decorated tiles of several sizes, miniature pots, mostly jugs and pitchers (one-to-two inches high), and two-inch diameter bowls.

Willy spray-glazes most of the standard ware except for interiors of closed forms, which are poured, and dinnerware, which is dipped and poured by students or employees. Willy decorates some of the standard ware in his personal style, and some pieces are decorated by the students and employees with simple brushwork patterns. The technique used most for this ware is glaze trailing on bisque, done by the students and employees. Using a rubber bulb filled with thick glaze (white or colored with iron or cobalt), complex patterns are built up with quick, simple strokes. Several basic patterns are adaptable to various sizes and shapes, and these are usually followed rather closely. Some of the more skilled and experienced decorators, however, tend to evolve variations of their own, especially on larger pieces, although these too remain within the clearly identifiable studio style.

The standard ware is well-crafted, skillfully decorated, and a high degree of uniformity is maintained, even though many

Slab-built bottle with thrown top, brush decoration in cobalt blue on white glaze 9″ (23 cm) high.

people are involved. Normally, the person who threw a pot will also trim and attach handles, knobs, etc., but there is no attempt to follow through with decoration, which is often done by someone else. Some variations are evident in throwing skill, and some of the potters pull handles better or have a more deft and lively touch with glaze trailing, but a high standard is consistently maintained.

Individual work. The individual pottery made by Elly and Willy is richly varied, but always made in series. They are always experimenting with new forms, materials, techniques, and glazes, but also continuing some forms and ideas with variations over the years. Others may be tried once or twice, then abandoned—sometimes simply because they do not sell, or the reality has not equaled the excitement of the inspiration, or the idea no longer interests them.

From the Kuchs' work of the last few years, it would be possible to pick a large group of pots that would show a logical progression of ideas through many variations, exploring nuances of form and proportion and decorative motifs and glazes. It would be equally possible to select another group of seemingly unrelated pieces, the results of experimental digressions that often do not obviously become part of the mainstream development. Yet these too, in addition to their significance as individual pieces, contribute in more subtle ways to shaping the Kuchs' evolution as artists.

Most of their individual work consists of pots that, while definitely vessels, tend to be more decorative than specifically functional in intent. Myriad bottle and vase forms predominate, although bowls, plates, and covered jars are also common. In addition, they make series of small sculptures that explore certain techniques and formal ideas in purely abstract terms. The pots tend to be smooth, precise, gracefully proportioned, and flawlessly finished, yet still warm and lively. There is great variety, however, and rougher, looser, more casual, erratic, or whimsical pieces can always be seen.

Much of their work is a joint effort: made by Elly, glazed and decorated by Willy. All of the individual pots and small sculptures are made by Elly, using a variety of techniques, including throwing, slab building, and combinations of these with press-molded or extruded elements. Some types of hand-built pots are almost always decorated by Elly with impressed or applied designs, normally done before, or incorporated into, the forming process. Willy, who originally wanted to be a painter, does all the brush decoration on pots made by Elly (as well as some of those from the standard production). He also does some incised decoration, often using a stylus to develop some of the themes he uses in brush decoration, but achieving very different effects. There is a lively inventive quality in the decoration of both Elly and Willy that is sometimes bold and vigorous, sometimes subtle and delicate, often light and fanciful. Frequently used techniques or motifs still retain freshness, and new ideas and surprising variations of old ones continually enliven their work.

Their personalities and ways of working are quite different. Willy is excited, exuberant, full of nervous energy, impatient, and very fast. Elly is calm, poised, and relatively slow but efficient in her work. However, a disparity never exists between potter and painter, between form and decoration. They work beautifully as a team with great respect for each other, and neither seems to feel

Elly:
The workshop production gives us a financial basis that allows Willy and me complete freedom in what we make. The only compromise is that we can't work alone. Our customers are pleased with the many new ideas in our work and gladly accept most of them, but also want a certain continuity. So some forms and decoration remain the same (with small variations) over a long period.

Flask-shaped bottles made by Elly and decorated by Willy. This basic shape has been made in different sizes with variations in form and decoration over a long period. All are about 11'' (28 cm) high.

Unglazed except for interior and lip; incised decoration accented with iron oxide.

Decoration in black on white background, overlapping poured glazes.

Black glaze with brush decoration in iron red.

132

Iron red glaze, decoration in
black on unglazed band.

134

any loss in relinquishing part of the work on a pot to the other. Although each has specific individual strengths, their collaboration, based on shared ideas and values and more than 25 years of growing and evolving together, goes much deeper than a mere division of labor. They discuss their work in detail, criticizing and praising each other freely. Through joint effort and mutual stimulation, they achieve richness, variety, and strength that neither would have working alone.

Architectural ceramics. During the late 1960s and early 1970s architectural commissions comprised almost half the volume of the studio production and included murals for schools, kindergartens, autobahn restaurants, and other public buildings as well as interior and exterior walls in private homes. They range from subtle impressed and incised patterns in unglazed reduced stoneware to the bright, shiny primary colors of low-temperature oxidation glazes. Decorative patterns are sometimes bold and simple, sometimes complex and subtle. Some feature deep relief, while others painted on commercial tiles are perfectly smooth and flat. Elly and Willy have also made fountains (notably one in front of the toy museum in Nürnberg), large planters, and other decorative architectural ceramics.

The first murals were made in collaboration with painters who obtained the commissions and developed the design, while Willy provided the facilities and technical expertise to help them realize the concept in clay. In later years most commission work was designed and executed by Willy, although collaborative projects were still occasionally undertaken until recently. In the last two years Willy has preferred to concentrate on pottery and has accepted very few architectural commissions.

Left
Wall of large unglazed tiles in private home, impressed, incised, and combed patterns.

Opposite page
Detail of wall.

CLAY AND GLAZE FORMULAS

The following are formulas for some of the clay bodies and glazes used in the potteries discussed in the text. They are offered with comments, descriptions, and advice from the potters who use them. The names of the glazes are those used by the individual potters and are either simply descriptive or refer to their origins or development. Where important, particular brand-name materials have been specified, and it may not always be possible to find comparable substitutes. Generally, American terminology and cone numbers are used except in the Casson and Kuch formulas, which refer to Orton standard (large) cones. Harrison cone numbers are equivalent, while Seger cone numbers roughly correspond to the next higher Orton number.

It should be remembered that these formulas have been developed for particular situations and although they may give excellent results under widely differing conditions, there are many variables, both technical and personal, that affect working qualities and fired appearance, so that it may be difficult or even impossible to achieve comparable results. Differences in raw materials, methods of mixing, firing variables such as fuel, kiln atmosphere, heating and cooling cycles, as well as the manner and thickness of glaze application and the clay body over which a glaze is used, are all important factors. Some experimentation and alteration may be necessary to suit varying conditions or individual preferences.

KARL CHRISTIANSEN

Stoneware Clay Body

500	A.P. Green fireclay
240	Hawthorne fireclay
100	Ball clay (Kentucky O.M. #4)
50	Feldspar

Cone 10 Reduction Glazes

Big Two (gray-white)

950	Potash feldspar
450	Kaolin
50	Flint
150	Cornwall stone
25	Zinc oxide
50	Bone ash
250	Dolomite

Ethel's Red (Strong iron red)

1850	Potash feldspar
850	Flint
100	Whiting
300	Kaolin
500	Dolomite
350	Bone ash
150	Bentonite
325	Red iron oxide

Michigan Blue

800	Michigan or Albany slip
700	Potash feldspar
100	Bone ash
200	Whiting
300	Flint
15	Cobalt carbonate

Standard Stoneware Clay Body for Throwing

- 38.7 Ball clay (English China clay's S.M.D.)
- 33.8 Fire clay
- 12.7 Red earthenware clay (high firing)
- 6.4 Silica sand
- 4.2 Potash feldspar
- 4.2 Flint (80 mesh)

Porcelain Body

- 57.2 China clay (English China clay's porcelain China clay)
- 28.5 Potash feldspar
- 14.3 Flint
- 3%–5% Bentonite

Body is aged at least six months before using.

Seger Cone 10 Reduction Glazes

(Seger cone 10 is comparable to Orton cone 11.)

Tenmoku (Black/brown)
- 720 Cornwall stone
- 127 Whiting
- 68 China clay
- 35 Crushed iron scales
- 36 Iron spangles
- 15 Red iron spangles

Magnesium Green
- 623 Cornwall stone
- 132 Whiting
- 75 Ball clay
- 113 China clay
- 37 Magnesium carbonate
- 20 Red iron oxide

Porcelain Glaze (Blue/green)
- 463 Potash feldspar
- 170 Flint
- 134 Whiting
- 98 China clay
- 30 Talc
- 92 Barium carbonate
- 13 Red iron oxide

Dry Ash Glaze
- 50 Wood ash
- 25 Ball clay
- 25 China clay

Ash of various origins has been used, both washed and unwashed. Washed ash behaves more predictably. More shine can be had by increasing ball clay to 40–45 and decreasing china clay.

I rarely glaze directly over a plain surface. Rather, all my pots have been embellished with various coatings of slips done in the raw stages that greatly alter the glaze results, I rarely, if ever, use just one glaze alone on a given pot. Instead, two, three, or four glazes are thinly applied in rapid order over each other to achieve a depth and transparency, revealing, yet sometimes partially masking, the previously done slip work. So, my glaze formulas are only parts of a composition. No particular piece is enough to voice the complete work, but each adds to a coherent whole with results unlike any of the glazes used alone. The firing cycle is about 30 hours to cone 10, with alternating one-hour periods of heavy and medium reduction beginning at 1850° F and continuing to maximum temperature, followed by a slow 30-hour cooling.

Stoneware Clay Body

200	Cedar Heights Goldart stoneware clay
75	A.P. Green fireclay
25	Kentucky ball clay (O.M. # 4)
25	Grog (20–28 mesh)
12	Potash feldspar
9	Flint

Basic White Slip (For decorating on wet to leather-hard pots.)

25	Potash feldspar
25	Kentucky ball clay (O.M. # 4)
25	Kamec kaolin
25	Flint
4.5	Borax

Slip Colorants

Rich red-brown; 8% Red iron oxide
Brilliant red–green: 15% Copper carbonate
Pearl gray-green: 4% Nickel oxide
Flesh pink, mauve: 4% Chrome oxide

Color Washes (For decoration over raw glaze—colors vary with glaze beneath.)

Blue-black (mixed with water only):   10 Albany slip
                                         1 Cobalt carbonate

The following are mixed with celadon glaze as a flux (roughly 2 tablespoons oxide to 1 tablespoon glaze and enough water for desired fluidity.)

Rust-plum:	Iron oxide
Rust-gold:	10 Iron oxide
	5 Rutile
Green-red, mauve:	Copper carbonate
Purple-red:	10 Copper carbonate
	1 Cobalt carbonate
Dark rich brown-red:	10 Copper carbonate
	1 Iron oxide

Cone 10 Reduction Glazes

C7-10 Celadon (Brilliant with fine bubbles, exceptional color responses.)
- 280 Soda feldspar (#56 or Kona F-4)
- 20 Whiting
- 40 Gerstley borate
- 60 Flint
- 20 Bone ash
- 20 Zinc oxide

Used plain and with the following colorants:
- 2% Black iron oxide
- 1% Rutile and 1% Red iron oxide
- 4% Rutile and 1% Red iron oxide
- ½% Cobalt carbonate and 1% Red iron oxide

C7 Celadon (More subdued than C7-10.)
- 280 Potash feldspar (Clinchfield or Bell)
- 40 Whiting
- 40 Kamec kaolin
- 40 Gerstley borate
- 40 Flint

Used plain and with 2% to 4% Red iron oxide for gray/green.

7G Sugary Alkaline Matt
- 280 Soda feldspar (Kona F-4)
- 120 Whiting
- 80 Kamec kaolin
- 80 Barium carbonate
- 16.8 Tin oxide

Used with the following colorants:

- 4% Rutile

- 2% Red iron oxide

- ½% Cobalt carbonate
- 1% Red iron oxide
- ½% Copper carbonate

Cone 10 Red Clay Slip Glazes

CH-18C (Yellow/tan matt)
- 240 Cedar Heights Redart clay
- 40 Spodumene
- 120 Whiting
- 40 Kamec kaolin

CH-18A (Dark green semi-matt)
- 280 Cedar Heights Redart clay
- 80 Whiting
- 40 Soda feldspar (Kona F-4)
- 20 Kamec kaolin

Stoneware Clay Body

    100   A.P. Green Fireclay
     50   Cedar Heights Goldart clay
     25   Kentucky ball clay (O.M. #4)
      6   Cedar Heights Redart clay
     12   Feldspar
      3   28 Mesh grog

An additional 9 pounds of grog is added for handbuilding.

Cone 10 Reduction Glazes

Nelson Test H (Gray-white satin matt, intense color development with oxide decoration. The ball clay and kaolin are eliminated for cone 8 firing.)

    5400   Soda feldspar
    5000   Potash feldspar
    1000   Ball clay
     600   Whiting
    2600   Flint
    1600   Barium carbonate
     800   Kaolin
    1000   Dolomite
     100   Red iron oxide
    1400   Bone ash
      40   Lepidolite
     400   Bentonite

Colorants:
Celadon: 2% Iron oxide
Iron red: 4% Iron oxide

Alfred Matt (Creamy, mottled tan.)

    2298   Potash feldspar
    3000   Cornwall stone
    2250   Spodumene
    5200   Dolomite
    3750   Edgar plastic kaolin
     956   Flint
        EPK has been eliminated and
        10% Nepheline syenite added for
        cone 8 firing.

Ellen's Halloween cone 6-8 (Rich orange-brown to speckled tan, much variety in surface.)

    5300   Custer feldspar
    2200   Whiting
    1600   Barium carbonate
     900   Kaolin (EPK)
     500   Yellow ochre
     200   Rutile

Cone 10 (Seger) Reduction Glazes

(Seger cone 10 1320°C) is comparable to Harrison or Orton cone 11.)

Speckled Glaze

490	Potash feldspar
275	Barium carbonate
90	Chalk (or whiting)
85	Kaolin
70	Flint
100	Titanium dioxide
60	Tin oxide

Good on porcelain and over iron engobe.

Matt White

340	Nepheline syenite
250	Kaolin
175	Flint
135	Dolomite
70	Potash feldspar
70	Zirconium oxide
60	Zinc oxide
55	Tin oxide

Good over iron bearing clay bodies.

Feldspar Glaze (Seger cone 10-11.)

1060	Soda feldspar
410	Kaolin
270	Flint
50	Dolomite
20	Zinc oxide
190	Chalk (or whiting)

Iron oxide decoration over this glaze produces a rich iron red. Willy sprays an additional thin coat of glaze over the decoration for a better surface.

The following two glazes are often used together on white stoneware or porcelain, the iron red dipped or poured over a first coat of celadon. The combination is good for wax-resist decoration. Gum should be added to the glaze.

Celadon

830	Soda Feldspar
90	Chalk (or whiting)
100	Flint
20	Iron oxide

Iron Red Glaze

698	Potash feldspar
1000	Flint
410	Bone ash
360	Dolomite
400	Ball clay
348	Iron oxide

Cone 10 (Seger) Oxidation Glaze

Black Glaze with Matt Crystals

750	Nepheline syenite
20	Zinc oxide
50	Dolomite
30	Chalk (or whiting)
70	White clay
80	Flint
40	Copper oxide
30	Vanadium oxide

BIBLIOGRAPHY

Books and articles written by the potters discussed in the text.

Caiger-Smith, Alan. *Tin Glaze Pottery in Europe and the Islamic World.* London: Faber and Faber. Atlantic Highlands, New Jersey: Humanities Press, 1974.

——. "Workshop/Aldermaston Pottery," *Ceramic Review*, No. 5, October, 1970.

Casson, Michael. "Ceramics and Education," *Ceramic Review*, No. 21, May-June, 1970.

——. "Decoration, Paper Resist," *Ceramic Review*, No. 6, 1971.

——. *The Craft of the Potter.* London: British Broadcasting Corporation, 1977.

——. *Pottery in Britain Today.* London: Tiranti. Levittown, New York: Transatlantic Press, 1967.

Glick, John. "Some Proposals Concerning the Use of Waste Heat," *Studio Potter Magazine*, Summer, 1975.

——. "Studio Management," *Studio Potter Magazine*, Summer, 1973 and Winter, 1973-74.

Interviews with Alan Caiger-Smith and Michael Casson appear in *Potters on Pottery* by Elisabeth Cameron and Philippa Lewis. London: Carter Nash Cameron. New York: St. Martin's Press, 1976.

INDEX

Edited by Donna Wilkinson
Designed by Bob Fillie
Graphic Production by Ellen Greene